... BUT YOU CAN'T ENSLAVE MY THINKING ...

A Novel of African American Intellect

Jaye Swift

jayeswift@yahoo.com
Caroline.wolf@yahoo.com
First Edition, First Printing
Typed by: Caroline Wolf
Front & Rear Cover Photo: Jesselee Baines III
Front & Rear Cover design: Caroline Wolf

Order this book online at www.trafford.com
or email orders@trafford.com

Most Trafford titles are also available at major online book retailers.

Printed in Victoria, BC, Canada.

ISBN: 978-1-4269-3275-5 (sc)
ISBN: 978-1-4269-3276-2 (hc)
ISBN: 978-1-4269-3277-9 (e)

Library of Congress Control Number: 2010907071

Our mission is to efficiently provide the world's finest, most comprehensive book publishing service, enabling every author to experience success. To find out how to publish your book, your way, and have it available worldwide, visit us online at www.trafford.com

Trafford rev. 5/27/2010

 www.trafford.com

North America & international
toll-free: 1 888 232 4444 (USA & Canada)
phone: 250 383 6864 • fax: 812 355 4082

Philosophical systems are almost never the work of young men, because philosophy is a subject in which maturity of ideas comes with experience. But there have always been prodigies in subjects like chess, mathematics and music in which the structural relations are a kind with which the mind does well even before exposed to the ordinary experiences of life.

The term Philosophes can not be translated as "philosophers" because the thinkers to whom it is referred - eloquent and devastating critics of the old regime - were not philosophers in any strict sense, but rather students of society who have analyzed its evils and advocated reforms.

They were apostles of an 18th century movement identified as "the enlightenment". The thinkers of the age of reason. Poverty is not the concern of the "well to do", for it is mainly the consequence of improvidence, shiftlessness, immorality, and slothfulness.

Table of Contents

"What is a disaster pornography?
Africans define it as Western media's habit of blacking out ... Africa's stock market, cell phones, heart surgeries, the soaring literacy, and increasing democratization, while ... Gleefully exhibiting, and parading its ... genocides, armed conflicts & children soldiers, foreign debts, hunger, disease and backwardness."
Gbemisola Olujobi, Nigerian journalist

"One thing [African people] need is better PR ... If people in this country think of Africa as a place with kids and flies swarming around their heads ... then they won't understand that these people are you and you are them."
Don Cheadle, actor

"If I didn't find a way to separate my feelings, I'd have been crying the entire month I was in Africa. I see myself in all these girls, their struggles, and hardships that just seems unbearable. I have nothing but respect for them. I can't understand how someone who's been there can't want to reach back and do something."
Oprah Winfrey

"It's Africa's time; people holler out the [name] Africa like there's one place. Man, there's a thousand places. There's not just one Africa. I've never felt so positive about the future there, as I do now. We just have to help get it together."
Quincy Jones

"By not averting these colossal human tragedies (such as in Rwanda, Somalia and Liberia) African leaders have failed the people of Africa, the international community, and the United Nations has failed them."
Kofi Annan, former General Secretary of UN

"I love Africa. We go to Africa a lot. I take my children on vacation there all the time. We go to Johannesburg, Sun City, simulator rides, the movies, the record shops, candy shops, the bookstore, the wave pool. That's the part of Africa I want more people to see. The myth isn't true; [Africa] is lovely, and beautiful."
Michael Jackson

"We need each other. African-Americans should have a special appreciation for the relationship between the U.S. and Africa. Nigeria supplies about 10% of your oil, but the need for each other is thicker than oil."
Kenneth Kaunda, former President of Zambia

Why African-Americans are relevant in America today..?

We as African-Americans are in another one of our periods of occupation.

Ours is a history of occupations. Stretching back over the centuries, the Rothschild's, the Jackson's, the Lincolns, the Roosevelt's, J. Edgar Hoover, the stock market crash, the C.I.A. the F.B.I, for a short period of time… segregation, and now this time again, the Bush's…Yet, the African-Americans remain….

The Blacks remain….
Why ?...

Because over the centuries we've learned how to survive conquest.

Sometimes by fighting back, but more often by adapting to the ways of the conqueror.
You say we are supine, "a race of slaves". Not so I say… Never forget our pride!!! We are large in numbers… and powerful enough to be dangerous to the conqueror.
Why do we remain? …Why were we not decimated?
The answer is… That each succeeding wave of conquerors, discovered that the enslaving of the African American, the burning, the pillaging, the raping, and the looting of Africa – all of this was only the first step in conquest. Someone had to re-build the country… Someone was needed to till the fields, and bring in the harvest required to feed the conqueror. And Someone else was needed to serve as the buffer, to protect the conquered from the conqueror. This is what the "African-Americans" have done.
Over the centuries we developed certain skills, without selling ourselves to the victors. We've learned how to blunt their assault. We've learned how to lead without appearing to lead. We've learned when to move forward, and when to retreat. What you must understand is that for most conquerors… "Conquest" is an end in itself… ,but for us… for an

"African-American" it's only the beginning. But now, at this stage, in the new millennium the twenty first century.

What do we do?...

WE WAIT...

...But waiting does not mean we are doing nothing.

These structures around the city are less than 500 years old. The oppressed, (be they slaves, or natives) built these, and structures before these. Structures are perishable, buildings come down, and skyscrapers go up. High-rise apartment buildings, yet another structure. The wealthy insists on building them, and we cannot stop them.

They are the oppressors...

But what we can do is... make certain that "African American" laborers are employed to put up these buildings. "BLACK" masons, "BLACK" plumbers, "BLACK" electricians "African-Americans" feeding their African-American families, on high government wages.

Higher wages ever dreamt of in captivity.

Let them build their skyscrapers, and while they build them, we will continue to grow.

In what sense, you ask?

The answer is: That "African Americans" breed faster than they expect us to. Higher wages lead to larger "African-American" families.

In time we will be the majority – then we will vote their asses into the ocean... Enter

"Barack Obama".

BLACK
LIBERATION
ORGANIZATION
OVERCOMING
DISCRIMINATION....

West African cultures believe that a person would ultimately join the company of his ancestors after death and would in turn be deified by his descendants.

The associated belief that each person carries within the soul, the souls of those preceded him.

And each person is a living part of a larger ancestral soul.

This belief system enables them not only to endure but also to rise above the suffering and indignity forced upon them.

Slavery... where were we before... where are we now...

I was reading historic literature on the system of "Royal Absolutism", where the king was in theory, and in fact an autocrat. Responsible to God alone. (Such as Louis XIV of France). He was the supreme and only lawgiver.

Louis XIV squandered the resources of this realm, in his passion for military conquests. He possessed the strongest generals, and army. That... in 1667 he marched in, and laid claim to the rich Spanish Netherlands. The Dutch then formed an alliance with England, and Sweden, and forced Louis XIV to withdraw. He inturn invaded the Dutch provinces. So.. William of Orange, with the aid of his old enemies, the Spanish, and Austrian Hapsburgs, enabled them to "checkmate" Louis XIV.

William of Orange, and his wife Mary, (William & Mary University) who replaced King James II on the throne of England, led an anti-French coalition consisting of England, Holland, Austria, Spain, Sweden and a few German states, and forced him to sign a compromised peace treaty, in which he gained little.

I observed a few things in this literature,
For instance:

(1) Africa was not included in this history, which could have presented her as a humanized civilization, worthy of natural respect.

(2) "In the absence of Africa". All of these countries, under a "monarch leadership", were jockeying for 1st place position, as the dominate world power, and the leader in the advancement of modern civilization as they new it.

(3) All of these countries went to war with each other. Fought, Won, and Lost battles, but signed peace treaties with little animosity, for the benefit of the bigger picture... The advancement of the free world.

(4) These countries learned the importance Of well developed navies, to protect their Borders.

(5) They learned from one another's advancement in technology. They shared information, strategies, and formulas for scientific solutions, with each other.

(6) They all practiced a sovereign government, "Royal Absolutism" in the beginning. Spain had.. Phillip V, Austria had Maria Theresa, England had Queen Elizabeth, and King James I and II, France had Louis XIII and XIV, Prussia had Hohenzollern, Scotland had James Stuart, Great Britain had King George III, Russia had Peter the Great. (who traveling as plain ole Peter Mikilailov, had worked as a common ships carpenter, in order to learn the Dutch methods of shipbuilding). Sweden had Gustavus Adolphus. Catherine the Great was a German princess. (Who married the heir to the Russian crown).

Poland.. Without natural borders to aid in its defense, was a handicapped nation. In addition it was dominated by reactionary nobility, (which meant.. they waited for something to happen before, implementing a strategy or a solution.) whose insistence on retaining its feudal liberties, (embarking on their right to fight wars) rendered the central government virtually powerless. The monarchy was elective, and the Poles usually could not agree on the choice of a king, from amongst their own faction (for too much internal bickering, and civil unrest). Only two native-born Poles had been elected to the throne in 200 years.

I've also observed "healthy wars", and healthy war strategies. (Relationship -building wars).

Nobility marrying nobility to secure their kingdoms advancement in wealth, Or advancement in dominance of power.

This interaction, I think, was very necessary to gain respect, and "AFRICA'S ABSENCE WAS DETRIMENTAL" to its own existence.

Why you ask?...

For the Europeans did not fear them.

I also believe the countries of Europe were wise to practice "Royal Absolutism". In the event of an emergency a decision can be brought forth swiftly. Had Africa practiced "Royal Absolutism" they could have prepared rapid strategies of defense.

In the early years, countries showed ruthlessness to kill, and a willingness to die for, execute, wage war on, battle against, or become the adversary of...anyone who spoke against their King, Queen, or their Country. "This too, was very, very important".

The absence of Africa in those battles… contributed to its appearance as nothing more than a tropical paradise. An island of wealth, and riches, ripe for their pillaging.

I believe that Africa had too many chiefs, and not enough Indians. Too many countries, with too many old traditions, and not enough thought to structure, or to modernize their continent.

I also believe that their inability to elect one sole ruler, led to what I like to call …

"Polandism": This is when a country's inability to consistently, and effectively elect a ruler, or advancement strategies, leads to Arrested Development.

As we know the continent of Africa is extremely plentiful, with maybe 53 countries. I believe that the internal bickering, and civil unrest, could have been ruled upon quickly, and laid to rest, had they practiced a sovereign government. Thus giving them opportunity to industrialize. I believe That lack of a navy to patrol it borders, was also a grave contribution to the inadequate defense of Africa. Had they practiced "healthy wars", and strategies they could have prevented the inevitable (they would have had experience in fights, battles, wars, and they wouldn't have been so astonished at people trying to enslave them.) ("a house divided against itself, shall soon crumble") ,or to para-phrase the oppressor…("United we stand, divided we fall") the enslavement of African-Americans.

Why was the enslavement of Africans inevitable?

Thomas Hobbs (1588-1679) composed the most penetrating, and influential justification of absolutism. Hobbs discovered what he believed to be the essential nature of man, when not restrained by law. Hobbs saw (man) "as a wolf to his fellow man", and… (mankind)… as essentially selfish, and cruel.

Before law, and authority came into existence, men lived under the adverse conditions of the state of nature. The second law of nature: (kill or be killed.) To create a workable society, and escape from the intolerable evils of the "state of nature," men surrendered all their rights, and powers to a sovereign government. (The first law of nature: Self preservation)

As civilizations moved forward the Europeans were encouraged by their monarchs to conquer, and retrieve treasures, to escalate the race for advancement, for their individual countries. (Which was the natural practice of their era.) As to be expected, giving the race for dominance, and power, the more gold, and silver a nation obtained, the more powerful it was thought of.. Many Europeans believed that "money is the sinews of war" (and, it is only the abundance of money in a country that determines its greatness, and power.) Jean Baptiste Colbert.

So when the Europeans ascended upon Africa they were not prepared for their findings. The profound excess of wealth, and riches far beyond their wildest imagination. Their eyes became greedy, their hearts larcenous, and staying true to their nature, with no law to restrain them, they ruthlessly slaughtered, and enslaved unsuspecting African villages.

The British for saw wealth in the land, agriculture (the gold, and diamond mines.) The Dutch, and the Portuguese (being not as cultured as the French and English,) sought wealth in the African people (the slave trade). The Spanish, and French soon followed suit. The French also invested value in African culture, and artifacts as well.

Kings, and Queens alike were captured, and tortured into submission. Princes, and Princesses, too, found themselves at the mercy of the treacherous. Where "mercy" was a foreign entity.

Their method of torture became common practice, and law, in the wilderness of North America for centuries. ...And I quote...

"You can tell the true content, and characters of a person on how they treat others they don't have to be nice to."

Let's fast forward to present day, 21st.century.

Let me just say for the record, in my opinion...

I don't think that slavery, and the oppression of

"African-Americans" would have lasted so long, had mother Africa not been so plentiful in her abundance of refined wealth.

Many nations have been like sucklings from her breast. (Great Britain, France, Spain, Portugal North America, South America by way of Spain, Jamaica, and the Virgin Islands by way of the British, and the Dutch). Just to name a few. I left the Dutch, and Portuguese for last, for I believe it was their "brainstorm" to start the slave trade.

When I look at Holland, and Brazil's growth in comparison with their European counterparts, I see them as critically underdeveloped. I like to think of it as justice for their hand in the slave trade.

When I look at "African-Americans" today I see collectively our wealth surpasses Holland's (again... justice).

In my opinion, had the Dutch, and the Portuguese invested wisely in the agriculture of "Mother Africa" they would've faired better, like their European counterparts. Slavery has been abolished 150 plus years, but "Mother Africa" is still fruitful to this day, still plentiful in her natural resources (justice).

Also, in my interaction, and relationships with today's Europeans, I find them sincerely apologetic for the role their ancestors played, in slavery. I believe, in my opinion that if they (today's Europeans) could do something about it they would. I also believe that, when African-American "artist" go to Europe they're held in high regards because of this.

In my opinion, reparations, or a formal apology could not come from the White House, or the United Nations, it would implicate too many important American forefathers (Washington, Adams, Jefferson, Madison, Monroe, Lee, Houston, Van Buren, Franklin, Stevenson, Bush, Grant, Lincoln, Roosevelt, Jackson, and Polk, just to name a few). To get a formal apology would admit to.. too much wrong doing. Which could lead to a conspiracy, which can cross over into "war crimes" committed by Europeans, as well as the United States, thus leading to lawsuits for "African-Americans" against all... showing profits from slavery. (Like the Jewish people did for the holocaust). Since "Mother Africa's" natural resources, and artifacts have been sprinkled throughout the world, that would be a lot of reparations. It would just be too much to give back, so they will not even consider opening that can of worms.

In my opinion, "African-Americans" are in the same state of mind donned pre-slavery Africans. We still live in a "Utopia state of mind". Full of luxuries, Leisure's, and Pleasantries with our tropical stimulants, (marijuana, ecstasy, cocaine, etc.) keeping us docile, tranquil and ignorant. Yes... IGNORANT!

How can we as a people (after 400 years of captivity & 65 years of drug addiction) consider putting foreign chemicals in our Holy Temple, (our bodies,) the body of the genetically superior!

Well... we used to be, but not any more. We used to own the fact that we were the physically superior, atheletic specimen, as an edge, and a plus for the "African-American". We've lost our edge, and we're losing our direction. By polluting our morals, our bodies, and our minds with chemical substances.

"African-American" women used to be the envy of all women. (The lips, the hips, the breast, the rest)...and fellows, do we really think our endowment is a race building issue? At the rate we're going; in let's say a 100 years we're going to be extinct. We're losing black people at an extremely alarming rate. To the PRISON systems, to DRUG abuse, to GANG violence , or to AIDS. We're killing ourselves off.

We're the new "CONFEDERATE SOLDIERS."

We're The new KKK.

Also we've become satisfied with the "pursuit of happiness" without obtainment, without possession.

We still possess riches collectively in abundance, we have no clue what to do with, except become the primary consumer for every enterprising merchant inside, and outside of the country, (houses, cars, clothes, liquor, rims, jewels).

Collectively we could fund our own country, if we possessed land the size of a Manhattan Island.

We still possess nobility. All the rap stars, movie stars, singers, athletes, (Oprah, Jordan, Magic, Jay-Z, Russell, 50Cent, DRE, Lil. Wayne, Shaqueal O'Neal, Reggie Bush, McNabb, Tomlinson, Cosby, Halle, Eddie, Griffey, Bonds, A-Rod, just to name a few) that have celebrity status. Just our nobility alone would be an extremely tremendous tourist attraction, and the world would flock to our country where ever it is.

We still possess no elected sovereign government of "African-Americans", by "African-Americans", for "African-Americans". We still possess internal bickering, and civil unrest. We still have no number 1 ruler, no autocrat, and no supreme and only law-giver. We still suffer from "Polandism" (we still possess reactionary leaders). We still possess no navy, no strategies for advancement. In fact, we rely on the very same government that enslaved, and tortured our ancestors for 400 years to protect us, and we expect them to be just with our health, wealth, and nobility. IGORANCE

We've acquired wealth without responsibility,

Intelligence without authority,

and ability without recognition.

In my opinion, all the world over would champion, "African-Americans", and the American government shaking of the hands, and putting this atrocity of slavery behind us. I think if black, and white inside America make peace, the world outside America could be at peace. I think tension mounts when European whites interact with blacks, until the initial introduction, and conversation. I think what happened, the atrocity of slavery was absurd, but I also think what we're asking for as payment for this act, is absurd... It's like; we want them to put themselves in slavery. It's not going to happen. The Asian tourists have somewhat shied away from dealing with blacks, in lieu of our history, they expect us to take to the streets in massacre of whites. So in truth, all races outside America, champion a compromise, or a harmonious solution, most African-Americans do, as well they just don't voice their opinion for fear of looking like an Uncle Tom. I just don't see it coming to pass, inside America, fore it's far too easy for both sides to rehash old grievances, and reopen old wounds, or dwell in the past. Unless we elect a black president.

Slavery: Where were we before, where are we now?

Where will we be in the future?

Why are we in a similar state of mind as pre-slavery Africans? The ineffective productivity, the arrested development, the reactionary leaders? The next 100 years may not be as generous if history repeats itself.

In conclusion: We need to change our political strategy. We need a government outside the American government, inside the United States . To keep an eye on the machinery known as the American justice system. We need to set up our own voting system in all the churches in our neighborhoods. We need to get candidates to run, and elect an "African-American" president for "African-Americans", outside the White House, inside th United States. We need our own government to keep their eyes on the machinery of the U.S. government. We don't need reactionary leaders waiting for something to happen, before they start marching, or thinking about solutions.

We need our own "African-American" "think-tanks". We need a 25-year project, a 50-year plan, and a 100-year strategy for the advancement of "African-Americans". We need to establish an "African-American" bank, to fund an "African-American" president. We need to get serious politically, about our future as a race, and a civilization.

A people will not look forward to posterity, if it has never looked backward to their ancestors.

The death of the tyrant is necessary to reassure those who fear that one day they will be punished for their daring attempts to sever their allegiance with the hierarchy, and also to terrify those who have not yet renounced the monarchy. A people cannot found liberty when it respects the memory of its chains.

Black
Liberation
Organization
Overcoming
Discrimination

When the band stops playing!

Poverty is not the concern of the "well to do", for it is mainly the consequence of the improvidence, the shiftless, the immorality, and the sloth.
This is the mind set of the wealthy…
When the curtain drops and the fans go home, when the entourage disperses and the groupies jump ship, when the lights come on and the janitors lock up,

What happens to your people?
The ones who took the bullet for you?
The ones who "bust they guns" for you?

Where do they go?
When there are no more shopping sprees and no more V.I.P.'s.
"Where ya men's 'n dem at now"?

Truth is, everybody can't be the star, and to just support those who are blessed with talent is a hypocrisy in every aspect of the word, to the black race.

What happens to the grandchildren and great-grandchildren of the victims of the drug dealers?
In order for Frank Lucas, Nicky Barnes, Rich Porter, and Freeway Rick to persevere, there had to be drug users.
In order for Rayful Edmonds and Guy Fisher, Fat cat Nichols, Pappy Mason to prosper there had to be "dope-fiends". Dope-fiends with kids, dope fiends with jobs, dope fiends with mortgages (rents), futures, dope fiends with functioning contributions to society, whose children's lives were destroyed, in the wake of an all out unsuspected chemical war, waged and engaged on the black future of America by the CIA.

The African American Children...

Where is their support system?

You see it would be easy to perpetuate the propaganda, that there is a grant here, and a scholarship there, for all blacks who want it.

Hind sights being 20/20, the recipients of these gifts, and grants were predestined.

So, to band wagon your support is only a facade, to mask the stroking of your own ego, so that now you can brag. ("Hey, look y'all, I backed a winner"). In actuality these scholars were already conditioned, and bred for college. Which just exhibits your opportunistic, blood-sucking nature, because they were winning without you.

In actuality, and in truth you have inherited, and exhibited, the characteristics, and traits of the oppressor.

But what of the African-Americans whose only inheritance is a "dependency gene pool"?

Where is their support system?

If you give them too many sodas, they're hooked on sodas. If you give them too many video games, they're hooked on video games. Too many shoes, they're hooked on shoes. Clothes, bottled water, sex. Hooked, hooked, and hooked.

What talk of these African-Americans?

What talk of these... whose legacy of dependency was handed down to them from generation to generation, from great-grandparents, to grandparents, to parents? The African-Americans, whose dependency gene pool gives them a chemical imbalance, which disables them, to form close ties, and relationships. A gene pool that hinders them from being able to love, and to trust fully, and completely. A gene pool that disables their temperamental skills, disabling them to control their anger, violence, or fits of rage.

What talk of them?

A gene pool that impairs, or slows their response, and reaction time. A gene pool that disfigures their ability to learn, to comprehend, to process information adequately.

Where is their support system?

Somehow this is acceptable to America. As long as we suffer in silence. As long as we go home, and be with our "a-alikes" (others like us). America has convinced itself that it's not that bad.

Americans are in a constant state of denial that any of this even happened at all. When in fact the conspirators were the FBI's co-intelligence under the direction, and supervision of J. Edgar Hoover, and his affiliates, at the CIA.

Dr. Martin Luther King Jr. was a genius, in the way he chose to expose America, for what it is, to the rest of the free world.

America tried to present itself as moral, and just, and fair to all African-Americans. The U.S. tried to say That we were lying, that we were over exaggerating. But...

Dr. King exposed the skeletons, in the American closet. Racism against blacks in this country. He revealed that he could not walk down a southern Alabama street without being attacked by police dogs, or sprayed with a fire hose. He revealed the extremely unlivable conditions, that we were forced to live in, in our neighborhoods, in this country. The cesspool like communities. The mis education, of the board of education.

This is why Hip Hop will continue to express the pain, and atrocities that has been afflicted on us for centuries. People around the world, now can listen to our words, and feel our pain, and anger in our lyrics. People around the world, can sympathize with us because they understand how the White Americans perform when they go to foreign countries.

Alas' we refuse to suffer in silence, and before we die we're going to make our presence felt.

Since we've acquired nothing, we have nothing to lose.

So please don't be surprised (while on our way to the grave) if we reach up and snatch one of you (bloodsucking, leeching ass, opportunistic, jovial, rich son's of bitches) into the grave along with us.

You may complain about us on the news. You may have discussions about us on your talk shows.

You may even belittle us, in private along side your "a-alikes". But ask yourself (truthfully), did you honestly try to help us? Yes.. You band wagoned the college crowd, but our kind ... we ain't going to college. Did you try to help Us?

We ain't the talented star, with hit records going platinum, we can't dribble a basketball, or throw a perfect spiral football

we aint marketable...

Did you try to help us ?

Where is our support system?

Someone once said (I forget who), if you don't vote, don't bitch about the government. The same goes for us. If you don't help us, (fine, we don't want your help.)

But don't bitch about us!!!

Don't bitch about us, when we wind up in your living room, in the middle of the night with a ski-mask on.. Don't bitch about us when you come home, and all your valuables have vanished...

Don't bitch about us!!!

Don't bitch about us!!!

Don't bitch about us!!!

You see, you can't kill us off ...and we ain't going anywhere. we're also breeding more like us everyday.

So keep looking over your shoulder, because we're coming.

And when the band stops playing, when the crowd disperses, when the lights come on... You become human again.

You become mortal again.

We the descendants of the wise, and noble peoples of hell's, find it no longer possible to suffer without cowardice, and self-contempt the cruel yoke of the American power which has weighed upon us for more than four centuries - a power which does not listen to reason and know no other law than its own will, which orders, and disposes everything despotically, and according to its own caprice. After this prolonged slavery, we have determined to take arms to avenge ourselves, and our country against a frightful tyranny, iniquitous in its very essence ...

See you soon.

Jaye Swift

Black
Liberation
Organization
Overcoming
Discrimination

TO: DR. WILLIAM H. COSBY JR. 'I mean the Cozzz...

Dear Dr. William H. Cosby Jr.

I understand that you have an issue with Hip Hop, and its impression on today's youth. Well, I'm a bit taken back, because... where was your voice, when JFK was assassinated in '1963, or in '1965 when Malcolm X was gunned down?
Where was your outraged voice in 1968 when Dr. King was senselessly murdered? Where was that fire when the "KKK" tried to march through Watts, and set off the Watts riot in (1965)? Where was your allegiance, when the police (in California, New York, Philadelphia, Texas, and Chicago), went on a hunting expedition, seeking out, and destroying "any, and all" African-Americans in black leather jackets, and black berets. Or with a tattoo that said "BLACK [anything] [Panthers, P. Stones, Spades]"? Where was that passion then? Where was that gumption when we mourned the loss of George Jackson, and the "Soledad-7"?
When Angela Davis was accused of kidnapping Patty Hearst? In 1971 when a top ranked "Black Panther", by the name of Fred Hampton, was riddled with bullets, while lying in bed unarmed in the wee hours of the morning in Chicago.

Where was your celebrity influence then?

I know you were around back then. I know because, we (African-Americans) supported you. We awed in amazement to your "I spy". We rose early Saturday morning to watch your "Fat Albert" and "The Cosby Kids" and please don't forget the "Brown Hornet". We (African-Americans) flocked to the movie theaters in support of your "Uptown Saturday Night". And did it again with "Let's Do It – Again".
I don't even want to talk about "Ghost Dad" and my kids.

Or how we rushed home on Thursday nights to have dinner with "The Huxtables". Week after week, year after year. For 8 years.

We were in disbelief when some young tramp claimed to be your illegitimate daughter...
And ...We all agonized over the brutal slaying of your only son, the terrific "Ennis Cosby".

Even after you "stiffed" the elementary school kids, who erected a mural to commemorate the success of "The Cosby Show". You exploited them by using the mural, and not pay its worth.

Still... we loved, and supported the "Jell-O Pudding Pop Dad".

But......

It appears we (the Hip Hop community) have fallen from grace. His Highness is displeased. We lowly peasants are uncultured. So show us.. oh mighty great one, show us something, Cozzzz.
Show us your "rally buttons" from way back.
Show us your fliers from the marches, the pictures with Black Activists, show us the documented, proof that you were there, in support of "The Movement". show us something that says, "you do have the audacity to have an opinion" on how we live our life today. Or to have an opinion on why Hip Hop needs to clean up it's act. Or talk about the revolution, show us because you supported your race, and the Revolution back then.

We've seen a young Jesse Jackson in a dashiki, and an Afro interacting with activist, mingling with Liberationists, protesting with other African-Americans, we want to see you, "oh, mighty great one".

I mean, you've been on TV 50 plus years, and famous for 60 years. So... Make us proud, show us your badges of honor. Did you even show up for the Million Man March?

You see, "Bill", Sir, no disrespect, but you would never be able to understand the betrayal.. Eleanor Bumpers felt. You couldn't possibly identify with Yu'cef Hawkins, or Abdouima. Have you even heard of Howard Beach, or Natasha Harlin? Do you even know the man's name, who set off the '92 riots?

But... enough about us low life's. Dr. Cosby: What's your legacy? What are you giving back to your race?

Hip Hop is a 50 billion dollar business. We (the Hip Hop community) have provided jobs for over millions of people worldwide.

So what's your contribution?

Everybody can't be a rap star. We're going to need some doctors and lawyers, teachers, computer programmers, and business men.

Where are the FREE "Cosby Computer Learning Centers"?
Everybody can't be a basketball, football, or baseball star. We're going to need some of that good ole Huxtable wisdom.
Help us out please.

A wise man once said: "If you don't vote, don't complain about the government." Well, Sir, if you refuse to help the youth, don't complain, when they become angry, desperate adults, ready to do harm to make a name for themselves.

Dr. Martin Luther King Jr., Leroy Jenkins, George Jackson, Nat Turner, Stokely Carmichael, H. Rap Brown, Joanne Chesimard aka Assata Shakur, and Afeni Shakur sacrificed their lives, and well being to give you an opportunity to succeed.
Their strategy worked. Now that you're successful with your hundreds of millions of dollars,

What are you willing to sacrifice to give others a chance to prosper.

If you don't of course you know, that makes you an opportunist, a pimp, a leech, a blood sucker of the poor righteous teachers the African-American people.

The fact remains every ghetto in America has a thriving economic base, grounded in crime. And when you have a majority of people living from check to check, with only two dollars above rent money to their name, it's more probable than not, that they will follow the money trail to crime. Because after everything is said and done, "money talks, and bullshit walks"

And...Hip Hop is the one legit way of side stepping the crime. Hip Hop is one way to live life with a clean slate, as apposed to dealing drugs.

You see, Dr. Cosby, it's a different world, from where you come from.

NOW!!! MR. COSBY WE'LL LET YOU DO THE JOKES, THE COURT JESTER-ING, THE STEPPING FETCHING,

AND YOU IN TURN, WILL LEAVE THE REAL...
"LIFE & DEATH" SITUATIONS OF,
THE TRUE AFRICAN-AMERICANS,
THE TRUE REVOLUTIONIST, AND
THE TRUE LIBERATIONS...
TO US...
THANK YOU...
Sincerely yours,
Jaye Swift

Black
Liberation
Organization
Overcoming
Discrimination

The Ten most important Supreme Court decisions in Black History.

(1) Dred Scott v. Sandford (1857)
Decreed a slave was his master's property and African Americans were not citizens; struck down the Missouri Compromise as unconstitutional.

(2) Civil Rights Cases (1883)
A number of cases are addressed under this Supreme court decision. Decided that the Civil Rights Act of 1875 (the last federal civil rights legislation until the Civil Rights Act of 1957) was unconstitutional. Allowed private sector segregation.

(3) Plessy v. Ferguson (1896)
The Court stated that segregation was legal and constitutional as long as "facilities were equal"—the famous "separate but equal" segregation policy.

(4) Powell v. Alabama (1932)
The Supreme Court overturned the "Scottsboro Boys'" convictions and guaranteed counsel in state and federal courts.

(5) Shelley v. Kraemer (1948)
The justices ruled that a court may not constitutionally enforce a "restrictive covenant" which prevents people of certain race from owning or occupying property.

(6) Brown v. Board of Education of Topeka (1954)
Reversed Plessy v. Ferguson "separate but equal" ruling. "[S]egregation [in public education] is a denial of the equal protection of the laws."

(7) Heart of Atlanta Motel, Inc. v. United States (1964)
This case challenged the constitutionality of the Civil Rights Act of 1964. The court ruled that the motel had no right "to select its guests as it sees fit, free from governmental regulation."

(8) Loving v. Virginia (1967)
This decision ruled that the prohibition on interracial marriage was unconstitutional. Sixteen states that still banned interracial marriage at the time were forced to revise their laws.

(9) Regents of the University of California v. Bakke (1978)
The decision stated that affirmative action was unfair if it lead to reverse discrimination.

(10) Grutter v. Bollinger (2003)
The decision upheld affirmative action's constitutionality in education, as long it employed a "highly individualized, holistic review of each applicant's file" and did not consider race as a factor in a "mechanical way."

Winter Fever

(Poetry in 17th century romanticism)

I rise in the dawn and smell the tension of the nature of the beast
Its howl ... Panasonic like... throughout the petrified forest
Its breath prickling amongst the limitations of my shawl

Will this be the dusk we fall prey to its devouring?
Not if we make hast in our abilities
I shudder at thoughts of dawn passing dusk

With no topped off partitions, or secured lens
But a skilled craftsman's' tool is active and accurate
If efficient in my dwelling then my goal is obtainable

The blond rays warm me over; it must be high noon now
Mystified and engulfed in the emerald littered carpet
The busy beaver I am not, for I've neglected my duties

Semi-conscious of the hawk circling above the glorious horizon,
Dissecting its route to consumption I cast down the die in competition
of escape
Fleeing for my lives faster and faster, I feel a presence hovering above my
shoulder

The razor-like claws lacerate my spine, as we lift off above the clouds
Then I am released, spiraling down, I crash, and ...
I die a million deaths in the dawn.

African-American Firsts

African-American Firsts: Government

* Local elected official: John Mercer Langston, 1855, town clerk of Brown helm Township, Ohio.

* State elected official: Alexander Lucius Twilight, 1836, the Vermont legislature.

* Mayor of major city: Carl Stokes, Cleveland, Ohio, 1967–1971.

* The first black woman to serve as a mayor of a major U.S. city was Sharon Pratt Dixon Kelly, Washington, DC, 1991–1995.

* Governor (appointed): P.B.S. Pinchback served as governor of Louisiana from Dec. 9, 1872–Jan. 13, 1873, during impeachment proceedings against the elected governor.

* Governor (elected): L. Douglas Wilder, Virginia, 1990–1994. The only other elected black governor has been Deval Patrick, Massachusetts, 2007–

* U.S. Representative: Joseph Rainey became a Congressman from South Carolina in 1870 and was re-elected four more times.

* The first black female U.S. Representative was Shirley Chisholm, Congresswoman from New York, 1969–1983.

* U.S. Senator: Hiram Revels became Senator from Mississippi from Feb. 25, 1870, to March 4, 1871, during Reconstruction.

* Edward Brooke became the first African-American Senator since Reconstruction, 1966–1979.

* Carol Mosely Braun became the first black woman Senator serving from 1992–1998 for the state of Illinois.

(There have only been a total of five black senators in U.S. history: the remaining two are Blanche K. Bruce [1875–1881] and Barack Obama (2005–).

* U.S. cabinet member: Robert C. Weaver, 1966–1968, Secretary of the Department of Housing and Urban Development under Lyndon Johnson.

* The first black female cabinet minister was Patricia Harris, 1977, Secretary of the Department of Housing and Urban Development under Jimmy Carter.

* U.S. Secretary of State: Gen. Colin Powell, 2001–2004. The first black female Secretary of State was Condoleezza Rice, 2005–.

* Major Party Nominee for President: Sen. Barack Obama, 2008. The Democratic Party selected him as its presidential nominee.

* U.S. President: Sen. Barack Obama, 2008. Obama defeated Sen. John McCain in the general election on Nov. 4, 2008.

African-American Firsts: Law

* Editor, Harvard Law Review: Charles Hamilton Houston, 1919.

* Barack Obama became the first President of the Harvard Law Review.

* Federal Judge: William Henry Hastie, 1946; Constance Baker Motley became the first black woman federal judge, 1966.

* U.S. Supreme Court Justice: Thurgood Marshall, 1967–1991. Clarence Thomas became the second African American to serve on the Court in 1991.

African-American Firsts: Diplomacy

* U.S. diplomat: Ebenezer D. Bassett, 1869, became minister-resident to Haiti; Patricia Harris became the first black female ambassador (1965; Luxembourg).

* U.S. Representative to the UN: Andrew Young (1977–1979).

* `Nobel Peace Prize winner: Ralph J. Bunche received the prize in 1950 for mediating the Arab-Israeli truce.
  Martin Luther King, Jr., became the second African-American Peace Prize winner in 1964. (See King's Nobel acceptance speech.)

African-American Firsts: Military

* Combat pilot: Georgia-born Eugene Jacques Bullard, 1917, denied entry into the U.S. Army Air Corps because of his race, served throughout World War I in the French Flying Corps. He received the Legion of Honor, France's highest honor, among many other decorations.

* First Congressional Medal of Honor winner: Sgt. William H. Carney for bravery during the Civil War. He received his Congressional Medal of Honor in 1900.

* General: Benjamin O. Davis, Sr., 1940–1948.

* Chairman of the Joint Chiefs of Staff: Colin Powell, 1989–1993.

African-American Firsts: Science and Medicine

* First patent holder: Thomas L. Jennings, 1821, for a dry-cleaning process. Sarah E. Goode, 1885, became the first African-American woman to receive a patent, for a bed that folded up into a cabinet.

* M.D. degree: James McCune Smith, 1837, University of Glasgow; Rebecca Lee Crumpler became the first black woman to receive an M.D. degree. She graduated from the New England Female Medical College in 1864.

* Inventor of the blood bank: Dr. Charles Drew, 1940.

* Heart surgery pioneer: Daniel Hale Williams, 1893.

* First astronaut: Robert H. Lawrence, Jr., 1967, was the first black astronaut, but he died in a plane crash during a training flight and never made it into space. Guion Bluford, 1983, became the first black astronaut to travel in space; Mae Jemison, 1992, became the first black female astronaut. Frederick D. Gregory, 1998, was the first African-American shuttle commander.

African-American Firsts: Scholarship

*   College graduate (B.A.): Alexander Lucius Twilight, 1823, Middlebury College; first black woman to receive a B.A. degree: Mary Jane Patterson, 1862, Oberlin College.

*   Ph.D.: Edward A. Bouchet, 1876, received a Ph.D. from Yale University. In 1921, three individuals became the first U.S. black women to earn Ph.D.s: Georgiana Simpson, University of Chicago; Sadie Tanner Mossell Alexander, University of Pennsylvania; and Eva Beatrice Dykes, Radcliffe College.

*   Rhodes Scholar: Alain L. Locke, 1907.

*   College president: Daniel A. Payne, 1856, Wilberforce University, Ohio.

*   Ivy League president: Ruth Simmons, 2001, Brown University.

See also Milestones in Black Education.

African-American Firsts: Literature

*   Novelist: Harriet Wilson, Our Nig (1859).

*   Poet: Lucy Terry, 1746, "Bar's Fight." It is her only surviving poem.

*   Poet (published): Phillis Wheatley, 1773, Poems on Various Subjects, Religious and Moral. Considered the founder of African-American literature.

*   Pulitzer Prize winner: Gwendolyn Brooks, 1950, won the Pulitzer Prize in poetry.

*   Pulitzer Prize winner in Drama: Charles Gordone, 1970, for his play No Place To Be Somebody.

*   Nobel Prize for Literature winner: Toni Morrison, 1993.

*   Poet Laureate: Robert Hayden, 1976–1978; first black woman Poet Laureate: Rita Dove, 1993–1995.

African-American Firsts: Music and Dance

* Member of the New York City Opera: Todd Duncan, 1945.

* Member of the Metropolitan Opera Company: Marian Anderson, 1955.

* Male Grammy Award winner: Count Basie, 1958.

* Female Grammy Award winner: Ella Fitzgerald, 1958.

* Principal dancer in a major dance company: Arthur Mitchell, 1959, New York City Ballet.

African-American Firsts: Film

* First Oscar: Hattie McDaniel, 1940, supporting actress, Gone with the Wind.

* Oscar, Best Actor/Actress: Sidney Poitier, 1963, Lilies of the Field; Halle Berry, 2001, Monster's Ball.

* Oscar, Best Actress Nominee: Dorothy Dandridge, 1954, Carmen Jones.

* Film director: Oscar Micheaux, 1919, wrote, directed, and produced The Homesteader, a feature film.

* Hollywood director: Gordon Parks directed and wrote The Learning Tree for Warner Brothers in 1969.

African-American Firsts: Television

* Network television show host: Nat King Cole, 1956, "The Nat King Cole Show"; Oprah Winfrey became the first black woman television host in 1986, "The Oprah Winfrey Show."

* Star of a network television show: Bill Cosby, 1965, "I Spy".

African-American Firsts: Sports

* Major league baseball player: Jackie Robinson, 1947, Brooklyn Dodgers.

* Elected to the Baseball Hall of Fame: Jackie Robinson, 1962.

* NFL quarterback: Willie Thrower, 1953.

* NFL football coach: Fritz Pollard, 1922–1937.

* Golf champion: Tiger Woods, 1997, won the Masters golf tournament.

* NHL hockey player: Willie O'Ree, 1958, Boston Bruins.1

* World cycling champion: Marshall W. "Major" Taylor, 1899.

* Tennis champion: Althea Gibson became the first black person to play in and win Wimbledon and the United States national tennis championship. She won both tournaments twice, in 1957 and 1958. In all, Gibson won 56 tournaments, including five Grand Slam singles events. The first black male champion was Arthur Ashe who won the 1968 U.S. Open, the 1970 Australian Open, and the 1975 Wimbledon championship.

* Heavyweight boxing champion: Jack Johnson, 1908.

* Olympic medalist (Summer games): George Poage, 1904, won two bronze medals in the 200 m hurdles and 400 m hurdles.

* Olympic gold medalist (Summer games): John Baxter "Doc" Taylor, 1908, won a gold medal as part of the 4 x 400 m relay team.

* Olympic gold medalist (Summer games; individual): DeHart Hubbard, 1924, for the long jump; the first woman was Alice Coachman, who won the high jump in 1948.

* Olympic medalist (Winter games): Debi Thomas, 1988, won the bronze in figure skating.

* Olympic gold medalist (Winter games): Vonetta Flowers, 2002, bobsled.

* Olympic gold medalist (Winter games; individual): Shani Davis, 2006, 1,000 m speedskating.

Other African-American Firsts

* Licensed Pilot: Bessie Coleman, 1921.

* Millionaire: Madame C. J. Walker.

* Billionaire: Robert Johnson, 2001, owner of Black Entertainment Television; Oprah Winfrey, 2003.

* Portrayal on a postage stamp: Booker T. Washington, 1940 (and also 1956).

* Miss America: Vanessa Williams, 1984, representing New York. When controversial photos surfaced and Williams resigned, Suzette Charles, the runner-up and also an African American, assumed the title. She represented New Jersey. Three additional African Americans have been Miss Americas: Debbye Turner (1990), Marjorie Vincent (1991), and Kimberly Aiken (1994).

* Explorer, North Pole: Matthew A. Henson, 1909, accompanied Robert E. Peary on the first successful U.S. expedition to the North Pole.

* Explorer, South Pole: George Gibbs, 1939–1941 accompanied Richard Byrd.

* Flight around the world: Barrington Irving, 2007, from Miami Gardens, Florida, flew a Columbia 400 plane named Inspiration around the world in 96 days, 150 hours (March 23-June 27).

Ignorance... A disease best inoculated with knowledge ...

What is a disease?
Disease: 1: An abnormal condition of the organism, or part that impairs normal physiological functioning, especially as a result of infection, inherent weakness, or environmental stress.
2: A condition, or tendency as of society regarded as abnormal, and harmful.

There are many kinds of diseases: sickle-cell, leukemia, cancer, polio, heart, lung-disease, and ignorance. Just to name a few. I care to expound on ignorance.

Ignorance is a legitimate infectious virus which has plagued today's African-Americans. Ignorance acts as any organism would: by penetrating vulnerable open wounds (in our community), met with little, or no resistance, hindering the normal progression of our people.

Ignorance can be transmitted in several fashions.
Infection: You can be infected with ignorance through unprotected sex, drug use, excessive drinking, through social association, as well as political.
Inheritance: You can inherit ignorance from your parents, since kids learn by example, more so than from instruction, From a parent. A parents' moral fiber is the condition of how a child will be raised. If a parent is consistently successful in its relationships with school, work, people, its children more than likely will become patient. If a parent is drunk, and abusive (which is displaying ignorance) the child is more likely to be violent, and abrasive.
Environmental: You can be affected by environmental ignorance almost every day. Let's say you're driving on the freeway, and an impatient driver decides he needs to be in the fast lane, from the far right lane. He hits his blinker, then immediately merges left, cutting off driver after driver.

Then "bam" he hits you! You have just been affected by "environmental ignorance". The same goes for school shootings at Columbine, and Virginia Tech. The students were going about their daily routine of education, and then bam, bam, bam…. "Environmental Ignorance".

But I'd like to focus more on infection: Infection implies two stages – healthy, then unhealthy… Transformation.

Ignorance of this nature is extremely damaging, for it can morph into a deep rooted ignorance. An ignorance so hideous, it destroys for centuries ("The gift that keeps on giving"), and the only way to get it out is to have it surgically removed ("make an incision at the point of entry, and have it sucked out, like the poison it is") or it'll just eat away at the central nervous system, until it corrodes its hosts' entire core, crippling its normal functioning abilities. This is the ignorance that has plagued the African-American for centuries.

Why, you may ask?

We as African- Americans find it hard to love ourselves as a people. We still bite into the white American propaganda, that we're second class citizens, that we're not as good white people. This is why when we do achieve a little individual success, or accumulate a little individual wealth, we express the need to look like we have money. We can't be happy as a normal person. Let's just say we'd rather be a star, not realizing we already are. And, if we have to live normal, and labor every day, for normal wages, we want all the luxuries that go along with it; all the bells and whistles. Now, I'm not saying we shouldn't strive, to be prosperous, but if we don't make the "A-list", it's not the end of the world. We still torment ourselves with the memory of slavery over 150 years ago. Over 150 years ago and it has still an affect on us? Damn! That's deep rooted ignorance. Most of us have never even seen a plantation. If you'd like to see a working plantation in progress, go to a prison – not County Jail or Youth Authority – prison. You work for $9 a month. And the prisons don't buy from outside. They make and grow everything on location. That's a 1,000 % profit. Yes, our ancestors were slaves, a long, long time ago, but look at us now… "We did that." We're not normal people. To survive 400 years of slavery and oppression then to persevere in the same country is not normal. Regular people don't do this. This is extraordinary, we can be proud of. I know my ancestors would be proud of you.

Why are "well to do" blacks so selfish with others in their race? And their favorite line is "I didn't get rich by giving money away".

Why are "well to do" blacks selfish?

"Well to do" blacks suffer from ignorance called "snobbism". They've fought hard to get the success they have, whatever it is. And if you can duplicate it, or them, they're not so special. Their value depreciates. It's like everybody has a goose that lays golden eggs. Also, they despise ones' inferiors, and their condescension arises from social or intellectual pretension.

It's the "Willie Lynch"-syndrome. Allow me to elaborate. Willie Lynch was a slave owner in the West Indies and he wrote letters to the slave owners in America on how to control their slaves, and run a strong plantation. He said: "You have to turn them against each other. You have to pit the light against the dark, the young against the old, the favored against the shunned, the house negro against the field negro. Simply: Divide and conquer." And the machinery of the government of America has perpetuated this strategy ever since. A mother, who needs a welfare-check against the baby's daddy, puts him out to receive one. A father struggles to make ends meet and his son who watches rap videos and wants to be "ballin'" and starts selling drugs. A grandmother, who favors the child with the good hair and light eyes as opposed to loving all her grandchildren equally. True story: I was out clubbing and I saw this very fine "sista". Long, straight, black hair down her back, body that won't quit and her ass was bananas. So I told her: "My African-American sistas are gorgeous!" She looked at me and said: "I'm not black, I am part Indian." So my retort was: "In-dee-end, you still a nigga."

This type of infection is called the "forbidden mirror". This beautiful lady would rather be a low budget mix of another race, than be a top of the line pure African American beauty queen. Anytime you say you're a percentage of another nationality then you're considered a cheapened, devalued version. It's like buying liquor: you want 100% proof, not the watered down 30% proof. And that's where she diluted her own worth. She can either be cheap champagne or expensive vodka.

Also, say you're out promoting your entrepreneurialism and you patronize African Americans. The male is reluctant to support you, because you look like him. And if he couldn't do it and you look like him, he doesn't believe you can do it. His attitude is 'how dare you try to be something, when he knows first hand you're not going to be successful. This is simply another case of the "forbidden mirror". Subconsciously you look too much like a loser, but – the loser you look like – is him...

How do we treat this disease? We have to treat ignorance with literacy. Willie Lynch once said "Black women are like mother horses: if you teach them to eat from your hand, they in turn will teach their colts to do the same." This is a horrible depiction of my Nubian goddesses and I'm appalled to have to relay such a demeaning statement, but it has a very minute fact in it.

Women who are on welfare solely with no other legit income, their children will have utilized the system in one way or another. Either they're incarcerated, or on welfare, or in foster care. There are success stories with public assistance - a lot of them, but right now we're treating ignorance.

Let's turn this negative into a positive, shall we? Let's give them a different hand to eat from. Let's give them the hand of confidence, and self esteem, or the hand of assurance and encouragement. Instead of 'dinner and a movie', do 'dinner and a museum'. Instead of chocolates and flowers give her a rare book or novel. Give her kids library cards. History books are boring unless you don't have to read them. Find movies that evolved from books and buy the book for the kids. Instead of Disney Land, go to Science Fairs. Join a book club, instead of a music club. If it becomes second nature to buy reading materials, she will teach her children to "read first and ask questions later". Decorate your house with encouragement and positive slogans. Use the power of positive thinking. Norman Vincent Peale suggests "if you can see it and you can believe in it, you can achieve it". Kids go to the fridge constantly; leave them a positive phrase in big letters for them to read every day, the same phrase. Something like "A quitter never wins, a winner never quits", or "Be a leader, not a follower", or even "Only dopes do dope". Then find positive acronyms. Find positive acronyms like P.E.A.C.E. Positive energy attracts creative evolution. There are many of them out there, or you can create you own.

It doesn't matter what you read, as long as you do read. The more you read the more you will aspire to be intellectual.

Literacy manifests information, information breeds knowledge, knowledge begets intellect and intellect bears wisdom.

In conclusion we have to give books the same quality time we give television. We want to watch the playoffs and the fights. And the ladies wants their shows, kids want their cartoons. If you watch TV for 9 hours, split that in half: 4 ½ for books, 4 ½ for TV. If you know your shows come on (in 3's or 4's) plan for it. Get your reading out of the way. The equivalent time allotted for three or four shows. Try this for one month straight; I guarantee you will see immaculate change.

But, to tune in is really just tuning out. As African Americans we need any and every advantage we can get. Because we're the future, we are the dream and we have the ability. So when opportunity knocks, we can answer.

What's the difference between a black man and a nigger?

What's the difference between:
"A black man and A Nigger"?

If they can ban the word "Nigger", can I sue America for defamation of character? Can I sue for four hundred years of pain, and suffering, or can I just sue for my years of suffering from birth to present day?

Can I sue America for all the times I've been insulted with malicious intent by the use of the "N-word" ?

For... it was with the governments consent that they legitimized the "N-word" and put it in the Webster's Dictionary anyway.

And I quote: "Nigger An ignorant person. A derogatory word, used towards blacks." So now they (the government) are teaching immigrants, and the millions of people who read the dictionary how to defile, defame, and degrade African-Americans

Yes, we use the "N-word" now, but history shows, even Africans-Americans, In past years, refrained from using it towards one another, unless it was intended to injure and/or cause psychological damage, and harm. (A technique learned, and used by slave owners and overseers).

The Hip Hop culture, "generation next", has given something important back to the black race...
What, you might ask?

Dignity, pride and self-respect.

How, you want to know?

They have successfully diluted and disabled one of the major silent weapons of the oppressor. That has attacked, and destroyed the psyche of African-Americans for generations. In my opinion, now, you don't have to hang your head in shame, when it's thrust upon you. In my opinion you don't have to slither, or slink away, when confronted with the ignorance of some racist asshole.

Now you don't have to black out and kill that devil, honky inbred, cracker mother fucker in a blind rage and wind up in prison.

Now everybody wants to be a "Nigga". Who, you say?

Black kids, white kids, Spanish kids, French kids, Swedish kids, German kids, rich kids, poor kids.
Kids who laugh a lot... tough kids, sissy kids, even kids with chicken pox...
Wants to be a "Nigga".

Why, some would inquire?

We as African-Americans, are the only race ever to persevere in the same country we were enslaved in.

Check the history books! The Israelites had to leave Egypt, the Jews had to leave Germany.

We went from slavery to bravery.
We took the pits and made a bowl of cherries. We took lemons and made lemonade. We took slave table scraps like the dark meat of the chicken, livers and gizzards and made soul food. The rave of all Europeans now. (Gumbo, oxtails, fatback, collard greens, monkey bread).

We took no instruments, just turntables and records and invented a new genre of music: "Hip Hop".

Hip Hop took us from Essence, Ebony and JET to URB. VIBE, Source, Rap pages, XXL, SPIN, Murder dog, Ozone, and Fresh coast Magazine.

From the tight shorts of Magic Johnson to the baggy shorts of Kobe Bryant. Hip Hop has raised the marketing value of the "African-American".

Pre: 1979 you could count the black millionaires, maybe 100: Post 1979 there are at least 100 black millionaires in almost every state.

Then if a white man calls me a "nigger"...
I used to wait outside, for him, and whip his ass everyday, then he'd be too scared, to come out of his house, so scared he'd move out of his favorite community, and into the suburbs. But that was then. Now... I say to him "No"... you're the nigger'. By the dictionary, and your own definition... you actually are the NIGGER.
Nigger = an ignorant person.

What's more ignorant than mispronouncing and misspelling the word "Niger, or negro" for four hundred years?

It's in the Bible: Acts: 13-1: "Now in the church was at Antioch there were certain prophets and teachers, Barnabas, Simeon, who was called "Niger", ministered to the Lord." Simeon, who was also a cousin of Joseph, Jesus' father by blood (Luke: 3-30). "Niger" was actually used to describe a person from Nigeria or Africa, which again leads back to dark skinned people.

Now the average southern redneck, American inbred's history is from Great Britain. Where as it stands today they were actually kicked out of the British controlled colonies, and Great Britain by the parliament because they were no longer assets to the British, and they were too poor to pay the parliament, the taxes they had thrust upon them, so they kicked them out. The poor, the sick, the criminals, the mentally ill, and the physically disabled.

We African-Americans were lured, and tricked with promises of gold for our labors, And then we were bound, and shipped out of our country.

They (the inbred) were ran out of their country, put on ships, bound for America. Kicked out.

The parliament of Great Britain discarded, rejected, and evicted the poor, the sick and the maimed, the mentally ill, the criminally insane.

With this history of their ancestors, they have no right to thumb their red noses at anyone.

These same people, who to this day, continue to sleep with their sisters, and make babies with their first cousins, All in the name of preserving the pure white master race.
They also live in trailer parks, collect welfare, smoke crystal methamphetamines, murder, rape, rob, steal, and make bastard children then go on the "Jerry Springer Show" and air their dirty laundry.

Now... if that ain't a nigger by your own definition, I don't know what is.

Question: So... what's the difference between a Blackman and a nigger?

Answer: The nigger is the one who doesn't want the "N-word" banned ... I personally hope they do it.

If they do I'm going to be looking into a law suit for defamation of character, conspiracy to mentally, emotionally, and psychologically torture me, to defile, and racially torment me with this word, by initially putting it in the dictionary in the first place.

For four hundred years they've used this word to describe my people, to summon my people, or to oppress my people.

That's a lot of "N-WORDS".

Pain, and suffering, my friends, pain, and suffering. Go ahead, let them ban it – I dare them.

Jaye Swift

Black
Liberation
Organization
Overcoming
Discrimination

NAS.... THE KING OF FLIP FLOP....

NAS... says... "hip hop is dead..."

Hip hop is dead to NAS, because he strayed so far from the Underground, that he didn't know how to get back. Then, and only then did he lose most of his true fans..

He went for the crossover audience not white, not black, just crossover. He couldn't get the exposure he wanted...
...OR WASN'T HAPPY WITH, the kind of exposure he was getting.

So he re-invented himself. He spread himself so thin that he couldn't pull himself together... And now no matter what he try's to do the Underground Hip Hop culture is like WTF?

I just want to know, How can the fans live by his words, or ride for his cause, and they don't, even know what his cause is.... He doesn't even know what his cause is, Or what side of the fence he's on.
He's an MC / gangster / drug dealer / abstract artist / actor / drug user / damn I'm confused.

This is why you rappers can't compare
Yourselves to 2pac. He had a direction, a sense of who he was. What his movement stood for. His knowledge of who the real enemy is. His passion for the liberation of blacks was so deep rooted. His skill of the arts. His lineage, and history he was a threat educated, or not...

You can't get any closer to what true Hip Hop is all about...
REVOLUTION AND LIBERATION

So on be half of the Underground, and my a-alikes KRS-1, Afrika Bambaata, hip hop lives.
...But its stunts like this new album titled...
"NIGGER..."

That makes us say WTF is he thinking?

Well this is just a publicity stunt,
A CHILD LIKE CRY FOR ATTENTION....
And we're going to have to pass..... on the new Nas album....
"Nah Fool" you're willing to... embarrass, and shame your own people, for a little fame. Your willing to play any role (no matter how detrimental) to get a chain.

Well NAS we're not going to play your little media games. Get some balls, and say what's really on your mind.

Like why would they put your nemesis in charge of a project he doesn't believe in. ,

Or how Jay-Z's CD "Kingdom Come" flopped, and he's allowed to put out "American Gangster"

Or he signed all those rappers to the roc and they all flopped...
Including "THE ROOTS"

Talk about how Russell Simmons used to be an Angel Dust-drug dealer then founded def jam...

Talk about how all def jam artist's lyrics contributed to the semi destruction of the psyche of the youth with it's lyrics all in the name of making a buck.

But don't drag us down with you...

Big JAYE SWIFT aka the Underground
        I am Hip Hop.... and....I'm alive..... PEACE...

ANALYZING, AND UNDERSTANDING: THE HUMAN MIND

According to John Locke (1632-1704) the mind at birth is like a blank tablet on which the experience gained through the senses is recorded. Locke maintained that, of itself, the mind has no innate power to grasp reality.

In acquiring knowledge the mind is not however completely passive, for reflection plays an important role, by the process of associating experiences received through different senses.
By extending the application of past experience to new situations, old ideas react on one another. Complex ideas are built up from simple ones, and can be broken down into the components of original sensory experiences, and reflections.

This was known as empiricism.

I would care to expound on Locke's theory for a moment. Understanding that this great mind had the disadvantage of being born in the sixteenth century, and having his essay published in 1670. I can clearly comprehend his primitive expression.

I in turn analyze the mind as a DNA-based computer....At birth both the mind, and the computer, are empty. Both are programmed by its parent, and siblings, and data is inputed.

Experience gained through different senses, if you connect a microphone, and camera to the computer, both can register, and process sound, volume, and exhibit photographic memory. If both are ignored, both will command the vessel that houses the mind to respond to neglect. Both have memory banks that through reflection both can extract data. Both can multi-task by opening more than one window at a time. Hence the expression "I'm thinking of a million things at once". Both strategize, and analyze information.

However, I'm not completely convinced with John Locke's theory...
"the mind has no innate power to grasp reality."

Let's analyze the youngest mind: an infant

Say an infant is fed, diapered, and laid to rest. When she is wet again, she will cry when needed to be changed, and the same if hungered.
This is routine for the next three months. Scheduled feedings, diaperings, baths, etc.

Alas she cries an un-scheduled cry, a cry totally out of the blue, the parent (let's say the father. I'm partial to fathers, me being one myself) hurries to tend to his daughter. Once he picks her up she stops crying. Father carries daughter while gathering the things he needs to assist him.

First he tries to feed her, but he can't seem to get the bottle to stay in. After a while he sees the problem, the baby's tongue is pushing the nipple out of her mouth. Father assesses, daughter is not hungry, she must be wet. Father puts daughter down to change her. Daughter starts to cry. Father removes diaper, to his surprise, daughter is not wet, but she's crying such a river. What could it be? Father picks daughter up to comfort her, daughter stops crying. Father, and daughter run through the cycle once more. Father assesses, daughter just wants to be held, and father obliges until daughter is comfortably off to sleep. What have we learned here?

1) Daughter (after three months on earth) has grasped the reality, that when she makes a certain sound people rush to accommodate her.

2) Daughter (after three months on earth) was aware of the sounds she made and had to choose one that would get her the results she needed.
   a) the gurgling sound (no)
   b) the baby-talking sound (no)
   c) the baby-laughing sound (no)
   d) the crying sound (yes)

3) Daughter (after three months on earth) was also aware of her necessities and assessed that she was
   a) wet (no)
   b) hungry (no)
   c) cold (no)
   d) lonely (yes)

4) Daughter (after three months on earth) can predict the actions, and re-actions of each parent.

5) Daughter (after three months on earth) is aware which parent will give her the results she's seeking, and chooses the opportune time to execute her plan.

Had this been the mother, who's mostly with daughter, she would've been wise to the game, and turned on the mobile, or put daughter in a bouncer, or swing.

Any deterrent to avoid constantly holding her, (so she can work around the house) and of course to avoid spoiling her.

Father did not, father was a willing participant, alas' daughter was victorious.

Daughter: assessed the situation
   1) had an objective
   2) devised a strategy
   3) contemplated a target
   4) gathered weapons, and ammunition
   5) waited for opportunity
   6) executed her plan

20,000 parents have been surveyed on Myspace in 2005... 87% said they have had this experience, thus proving the mind as innate power to grasp reality.

The mind has three states:
Consciousness, un-consciousness and sub-consciousness:

Conscious: Doing or acting with critical awareness. Having mental faculties undulled by sleep, faintness or stupor.

Consciousness: the quality or state of being aware, the totality of conscious states of an individual. The upper level of mental life of which the person is aware, as contrasted with unconscious processes.

Un: Having meaning positively opposite to that of the base word.
Un: Do the opposite of: reverse (a specified action) contrary to:

Unconsciousness: Doing or acting without critical awareness. Unaware. Instinct [sleepwalking]:

driving through a neighborhood, a ball bounces in front of you. Instinctively you hit the brakes, and check your rear view mirror all at once. A child comes from the sidewalk and retrieves the ball. Not thinking you check your rear-view mirror, again and continue on cautiously.

Sub: Under, below, secretly from below, beneath, bordering on below the surface.

Sub-consciousness: In my analysis:

I liken the sub-conscious to the internet experience. While browsing the internet you enter different websites, hundreds of windows are open to you. So you window shop, browse, research, download songs, etc. You've been to hundreds of sites, yet you have not signed up for anything specific. You're just on there having fun. You log off until the next day.
You log on the next day, and have "emails" from sites you never registered with. You have "POP UPS" trying to coherce you into purchasing something. Every hour you're flooded with 'junk mail,' and you're wondering 'how did they get your e-mail address?' You never registered with any of them.

Well, once you enter a website, cookies attach themselves to your signal, and you've opened a line for them to trace back to your ISP. It's like they follow you home, and live in your basement, and annoy the hell out of you, unless you go into your hard drive, and delete them.

Let's analyze the mature mind:

Your every day life occurrences: You go to school, or the mall, you have coffee, meet, and greet people, try on clothes, and shoes, eat lunch, talk on the cell phone, etc. You've done this on a regular basis for years. Meet your friends for dinner, go to baseball games, go swimming, jump off a diving board, or two. You're just living life, and having fun. Whatever you've done with your life you physically contacted, touched, tasted, smelled, heard, and seen life.

Now imagine you're sleeping, and in your dream you're falling (I won't pretend to interpret your dream), but you wake up, heart beating fast, sweating it's like you were really there, like it was so real.
Life's cookies have attached themselves to your sub-conscious hard drive. And while you were going about your day, something you encountered sent you a subliminal 'e-mail'. Whatever you've seen, read, smelled, tasted, or touched made an intimate impact on your subconcious, and you were unaware of it.

So when you went to "sleep" (I don't like to use this word "sleep," because 'sleep' in Biblical history meant death, and some even say "sleep is the cousin of death". I'd like to incorporate "rest" instead. Plus, as you know, the mind never sleeps),

Your consciousness checked your sub-conscious hard drive in your state of un-consciousness (rest) and opened a subliminal "e-mail" called "falling."

"Falling" has impacted your sub-conscious, whether you're diving, or just felt strongly about someone else's fall, or just looking over an edge, and thinking of falling.
"Falling" has impacted you beneath the surface of your consciousness, in your every day life.

As we go through life there are millions of subliminal messages around us. They're not aimed at any particular individual, but they are to a more demographical subject of a people.
Also they are meant to create a response. To manipulate you into a favorable choice, to hearde you in a direction like sheep or cattle. (to get you to react a certain way on a certain subject. It could be something as simple as buying refreshments, or a new car).

Give them drink, and give them games...
Keep them distracted, and entertained...
Because they're not educated, and they're un-informed.
And at this point they'll accept anything

But one must understand, Life, and its subliminal messages are the internet. The world, the country, the state, the county, and... the city we live in, and all we do.....is the internet.
The sub-conscious is just acting as the at home modem that connects us to the internet. The sub-conscious is not the internet, just the ISP (Internet Service Provider). And your dreams are your...
"e-mails" from interacting with life...
("the internet")

Have you ever had an idea just pop into your head?
For example: You're working in your office, and out of nowhere you picture a "Jamba Juice, or a Smoothie," and you want to taste the citrus acids on your tongue, the coolness of the juices. But... you're at work, and it's not break time yet, so you keep working. Then... while you're at your desk, you picture fruit: Sliced bananas, mangos, oranges, strawberries, pineapples, sliced watermelons, sitting on fresh white snow, and your mouth tries to taste it,
but it can't. And you think: "I can just sneak out for five minutes." But no..... it's not professional.
These are life's internet "pop-ups."
The sub-conscious has been sent a subliminal message, and the sub-consciousness has relayed the subliminal imagery message (re-processed in visualized format) to your state of consciousness, which in turn allows you to consciously visualize the recreation of the fruit in real time.

Hence the term "POP UP."

In my analysis I've dabbled in many stages of the mind, in its different states you've seen:
- Conscious interaction with the conscious (daughter and father)
- Sub-conscious interaction with the un-conscious (sleep walking)
- Conscious interaction with the un-conscious (driving)
- Conscious interaction with the sub-conscious (e-mails)
- Sub-conscious interaction with the conscious (pop-ups)

47

These are just a few stages of the human mind.
If you hold a jewelers loop to a perfect diamond, you probably still wouldn't see as many facets, and levels as the mind itself can contain.

Most Scientist' deter, or refrain from analyzing the mind, because of its complexities, and its instability.

Also, technology has yet to come up with a legitimate instrument to calibrate its levels of the mind accurately, thus becoming a non-exact science.

But through association, if we can begin to understand the similarities, we can comprehend the functions of the things that act, and respond similar, then we've begun to unravel one of life's most complex puzzles... THE HUMAN MIND.

FBIWARNING:

This is just a fundamental expression, and manifestation of my analysis for the average person to understand. Any reproduction, or duplication of the least without the express written consent of the author, and/or publisher is in direct violation of applicable laws.

This concludes my analysis:

The Black Issues Quiz

offers you an opportunity to test your knowledge on the people, places, issues, and history surrounding the struggle for academic equity. Each question is based on information published in the current or previous editions of Black Issues In Higher Education and is worth 10 points.

A perfect score of 100 grants membership in the prestigious and mythical Phi BIQeta Kappa honors society; a score of 80 to 90 grants membership in the Honor Society of BIQ Brains; a score of 60 to 70 grants membership in the Society of Not So BIQ Brains; and a score of 50 or below grants membership in the Reading Black Issues Is Fundamental program.

Think you are smart? Go ahead, give it a try? (Answer key appears at the bottom of the page.)

1) According to an analysis of Department of Education data, excluding Howard University, which Research I or II institution had the largest number of Black faculty members in the fall of 1995?

A -- University of Michigan-Ann Arbor
B -- University of Maryland-College Park
C -- Temple University
D -- Ohio State University

2) According to an analysis of Department of Education data, which Research I or II institution had the largest number of Hispanic faculty members in the fall of 1995?

A -- University of Texas-Austin
B -- Arizona State University
C -- University of Miami
D -- University of New Mexico-Main

3) According to National Science Foundation data, the top 100 research universities--among which there are no historically Black institutions--received how much money from 10 federal agencies in 1993-94?

A -- $600 million
B -- $140 million
C -- $12.7 billion
D -- $1.27 billion

4) According to National Science Foundation data, the top 81 historically Black colleges and universities received how much money from 10 federal agencies in 1993-94?

A -- $600 million
B -- $140 million
C -- $12.7 million
D -- $1.27 billion

5) According to Sallie Mae, what was the most popular method to pay for college in 1997?

A -- scholarships, grants, and work study
B -- parents' savings and income
C -- federally guaranteed student loans
D -- students' savings and income

6) According to a 1997 Center for Disease Control and Prevention report, how many African Americans have diabetes, either Type 1 or Type 2?

A -- 11.3 million
B -- 2.3 million
C -- 1.2 million
D -- 123,000

7) During the Orangeburg Massacre in 1968, students from which institution were killed by police gunfire?

A -- Kent State University
B -- University of California, Berkeley
C -- Jackson State University
D -- South Carolina State University

8) According to the 1997 Racial Report Card's analysis of National Collegiate Athletics Association (NCAA) data, what percentage of Division I athletics directors were African American men?

A -- 9.1 percent
B -- 17.3 percent
C -- 6.1 percent
D -- 23.9 percent

9) According to information from the U.S. bureau of Prisons and the U.S. Department of Education, in 1995, there were more Black men in prison cells than in college and university classrooms.

A -- True
B -- False

10) Dr. Steve Alexander Favors left his post as vice president for student affairs at Howard University to become the president of which historically Black institution?

A -- Dillard University
B -- Grambling State University
C -- Alabama A&M University
D -- Fisk University

Answers on page 138

A poem for Caroline

(in neo classicism 14th century)

Oh Caroline, oh Caroline, thy greatest love of mine
Thou, art the fairest, and, thy beauty hast no time.

Thou hast traveled the world over, for centuries, to and fro
Thy nose is artistically sculptured, by the hand of Van Gogh.

Thine eyes are emeralds, thy teeth, like pearls
Thy golden tresses cascade, longing to unfurl.

Thou hast eluded vagabonds, wagerers, and the poor
Many a battle has been lost for thy love, but thou alone winneth the war.

Laborers dreameth of thou companionship
Whilst wealthy mens keen sense of accomplishment.

Kings, and queens alike casteth claim upon thine heart
But lack of thy spirit, hath kingdoms throne apart.

Oh Caroline, oh Caroline, I matrimone, in lust
Let thy creation of the union be suckling from thou bust.

Please not heareth amongst the mute, that plagueth many others
For thou gaveth life infinite, allst he needeth ist a mother.

Please not turneth arctic, for an orphan, he is not
Just the sum of two energies colliding together, continuously in one spot.

Oh Caroline, oh Caroline, thy grandest obsession I find
I wagered with my life, alas I'm out of time.

Black History and Time Lines

The first African slaves arrive in Virginia.

1746
Lucy Terry, an enslaved person in 1746, becomes the earliest known black American poet when she writes about the last American Indian attack on her village of Deerfield, Massachusetts. Her poem, *Bar's Fight*, was not published until 1855.

1773
Phillis Wheatley
An illustration of Phillis Wheatley from her book
Phillis Wheatley's book Poems on Various Subjects, Religious and Moral is published, making her the first African American to do so.

1787
Slavery is made illegal in the Northwest Territory. The U.S Constitution states that Congress may not ban the slave trade until 1808.

1793
Eli Whitney's invention of the cotton gin greatly increases the demand for slave labor.

1793
Poster advertising $100 reward for runaway slaves from 1860.
A federal fugitive slave law is enacted, providing for the return slaves who had escaped and crossed state lines.

1800
Gabriel Prosser, an enslaved African-American blacksmith, organizes a slave revolt intending to march on Richmond, Virginia. The conspiracy is uncovered, and Prosser and a number of the rebels were hanged. Virginia's slave laws are consequently tightened.

1808
Congress bans the importation of slaves from Africa.

1820
The Missouri Compromise bans slavery north of the southern boundary of Missouri.

1822
Denmark Vesey, an enslaved African-American carpenter who had purchased his freedom, plans a slave revolt with the intent to lay siege on Charleston, South Carolina. The plot is discovered, and Vesey and 34 coconspirators were hanged.

1831
Nat Turner, an enslaved African-American preacher, leads the most significant slave uprising in American history. He and his band of followers launch a short, bloody, rebellion in Southampton County, Virginia. The militia quells the rebellion, and Turner is eventually hanged. As a consequence, Virginia institutes much stricter slave laws.

William Lloyd Garrison: begins publishing the Liberator, a weekly paper that advocates the complete abolition of slavery. He becomes one of the most famous figures in the abolitionist movement.

1846
Frederick Douglass
The Wilmot Proviso, introduced by Democratic representative David Wilmot of Pennsylvania, attempts to ban slavery in territory gained in the Mexican War. The proviso is blocked by Southerners, but continues to enflame the debate over slavery.

Frederick Douglass launches his abolitionist newspaper.

1849
Harriet Tubman escapes from slavery and becomes one of the most effective and celebrated leaders of the Underground Railroad.

1850
The continuing debate whether territory gained in the Mexican War should be open to slavery is decided in the Compromise of 1850: California is admitted as a free state, Utah and New Mexico territories are left to be

decided by popular sovereignty, and the slave trade in Washington, DC, is prohibited. It also establishes a much stricter fugitive slave law than the original, passed in 1793.

1852
Harriet Beecher Stowe's novel, Uncle Tom's Cabin is published. It becomes one of the most influential works to stir anti-slavery sentiments.

1854
Congress passes the Kansas-Nebraska Act, establishing the territories of Kansas and Nebraska. The legislation repeals the Missouri Compromise of 1820 and renews tensions between anti- and proslavery factions.

1857
Oil painting of Dred Scott
The Dred Scott case holds that Congress does not have the right to ban slavery in states and, furthermore, that slaves are not citizens.

1859
John Brown and 21 followers capture the federal arsenal at Harpers Ferry, Va. (now W. Va.), in an attempt to launch a slave revolt.

1861
The Confederacy is founded when the deep South secedes, and the Civil War begins.

1863
Slaves at Cumberland Landing, Va.
President Lincoln issues the Emancipation Proclamation, declaring "that all persons held as slaves" within the Confederate states "are, and henceforward shall be free."

1865
Congress establishes the Freedmen's Bureau to protect the rights of newly emancipated blacks (March).

The Civil War ends (April 9).

Lincoln is assassinated (April 14).

The Ku Klux Klan is formed in Tennessee by ex-Confederates (May).

Slavery in the United States is effectively ended when 250,000 slaves in Texas finally receive the news that the Civil War had ended two months earlier (June 19).

Thirteenth Amendment to the Constitution is ratified, prohibiting slavery (Dec. 6).

1865-1866
Black codes are passed by Southern states, drastically restricting the rights of newly freed slaves.

1867
A series of Reconstruction acts are passed, carving the former Confederacy into five military districts and guaranteeing the civil rights of freed slaves.

1868
Fourteenth Amendment to the Constitution is ratified, defining citizenship. Individuals born or naturalized in the United States are American citizens, including those born as slaves. This nullifies the Dred Scott Case (1857), which had ruled that blacks were not citizens.

1869
Howard University's law school becomes the country's first black law school.

1870
Hiram Revels
Fifteenth Amendment to the Constitution is ratified, giving blacks the right to vote.

Hiram Revels of Mississippi is elected the country's first African-American senator. During Reconstruction, sixteen blacks served in Congress and about 600 served in states legislatures.

1877
Reconstruction ends in the South. Federal attempts to provide some basic civil rights for African Americans quickly erode.

1879

The Black Exodus takes place, in which tens of thousands of African Americans migrated from southern states to Kansas.

1881

Spelman College, the first college for black women in the U.S., is founded by Sophia B. Packard and Harriet E. Giles.

Booker T. Washington founds the Tuskegee Normal and Industrial Institute in Alabama. The school becomes one of the leading schools of higher learning for African Americans, and stresses the practical application of knowledge. In 1896 George Washington Carver begins teaching there as director of the department of agricultural research, gaining an international reputation for his agricultural advances.

1882

The American Colonization Society, founded by Presbyterian minister Robert Finley, establishes the colony of Monrovia (which would eventually become the country of Liberia) in western Africa. The society contends that the immigration of blacks to Africa is an answer to the problem of slavery as well as to what it feels is the incompatibility of the races. Over the course of the next forty years, about 12,000 slaves are voluntarily relocated.

1896

Plessy v. Ferguson: This landmark Supreme Court decision holds that racial segregation is constitutional, paving the way for the repressive Jim Crow laws in the South.

1905

W.E.B. DuBois founds the Niagara movement, a forerunner to the NAACP. The movement is formed in part as a protest to Booker T. Washington's policy of accommodation to white society; the Niagara movement embraces a more radical approach, calling for immediate equality in all areas of American life.

1909

W.E.B. Du Bois

The National Association for the Advancement of Colored People is founded in New York by prominent black and white intellectuals and led by W.E.B. Du Bois. For the next half century, it would serve as the country's most influential African-American civil rights organization, dedicated to political equality and social justice. In 1910, its journal, The Crisis, was launched. Among its well known leaders were James Weldon Johnson, Ella Baker, Moorfield Storey, Walter White, Roy Wilkins, Benjamin Hooks, Myrlie Evers-Williams, Julian Bond, and Kwesi Mfume.

1914
Marcus Garvey establishes the Universal Negro Improvement Association, an influential black nationalist organization "to promote the spirit of race pride" and create a sense of worldwide unity among blacks.

1920s
The Harlem Renaissance flourishes in the 1920s and 1930s. This literary, artistic, and intellectual movement fosters a new black cultural identity.

1931
Scottsboro Boys
Nine black youths are indicted in Scottsboro, Ala., on charges of having raped two white women. Although the evidence was slim, the southern jury sentenced them to death. The Supreme Court overturns their convictions twice; each time Alabama retries them, finding them guilty. In a third trial, four of the Scottsboro boys are freed; but five are sentenced to long prison terms.

1947
Jackie Robinson breaks Major League Baseball's color barrier when he is signed to the Brooklyn Dodgers by Branch Rickey.

1948
WWI Black Soldiers
Although African Americans had participated in every major U.S. war, it was not until after World War II that President Harry S. Truman issues an executive order integrating the U.S. armed forces.

1952
Malcolm X becomes a minister of the Nation of Islam. Over the next several years his influence increases until he is one of the two most powerful members of the Black Muslims (the other was its leader, Elijah

Muhammad). A black nationalist and separatist movement, the Nation of Islam contends that only blacks can resolve the problems of blacks.

1954

Pictured from left to right: George E.C. Hayes, Thurgood Marshall, and James Nabrit Brown v. Board of Education of Topeka, Kans. declares that racial segregation in schools is unconstitutional (May 17).

1955

A young black boy, Emmett Till, is brutally murdered for allegedly whistling at a white woman in Mississippi. Two white men charged with the crime are acquitted by an all-white jury. They later boast about committing the murder. The public outrage generated by the case helps spur the civil rights movement (Aug.).

Rosa Parks refuses to give up her seat at the front of the "colored section" of a bus to a white passenger (Dec.1). In response to her arrest Montgomery's black community launch a successful year-long bus boycott. Montgomery's buses are desegregated on Dec. 21, 1956.

1957

The Little Rock Nine pictured with Daisy Bates, the president of the Arkansas NAACP.

The Little Rock Nine

The Southern Christian Leadership Conference (SCLC), a civil rights group, is established by Martin Luther King, Charles K. Steele, and Fred L. Shuttlesworth (Jan.-Feb.)

Nine black students are blocked from entering the school on the orders of Governor Orval Faubus. (Sept. 24). Federal troops and the National Guard are called to intervene on behalf of the students, who become known as the "Little Rock Nine." Despite a year of violent threats, several of the "Little Rock Nine" manage to graduate from Central High.

1960

Four black students in Greensboro, North Carolina, begin a sit-in at a segregated Woolworth's lunch counter (Feb. 1). Six months later the "Greensboro Four" are served lunch at the same Woolworth's counter. The event triggers many similar nonviolent protests throughout the South.

The Student Nonviolent Coordinating Committee (SNCC) is founded, providing young blacks with a place in the civil rights movement (April).

1961

Over the spring and summer, student volunteers begin taking bus trips through the South to test out new laws that prohibit segregation in interstate travel facilities, which includes bus and railway stations. Several of the groups of "freedom riders," as they are called, are attacked by angry mobs along the way. The program, sponsored by The Congress of Racial Equality (CORE) and the Student Nonviolent Coordinating Committee (SNCC), involves more than 1,000 volunteers, black and white.

1962

James Meredith becomes the first black student to enroll at the University of Mississippi (Oct. 1). President Kennedy sends 5,000 federal troops after rioting breaks out.

1963

Martin Luther King, Jr.

Martin Luther King is arrested and jailed during anti-segregation protests in Birmingham, Ala. He writes "Letter from Birmingham Jail," which advocated nonviolent civil disobedience.

The March on Washington for Jobs and Freedom is attended by about 250,000 people, the largest demonstration ever seen in the nation's capital. Martin Luther King delivers his famous "I Have a Dream" speech. The march builds momentum for civil rights legislation (Aug. 28).

Despite Governor George Wallace physically blocking their way, Vivian Malone and James Hood register for classes at the University of Alabama.

Four young black girls attending Sunday school are killed when a bomb explodes at the Sixteenth Street Baptist Church, a popular location for civil rights meetings. Riots erupt in Birmingham, leading to the deaths of two more black youths (Sept. 15).

1964

FBI photographs of Andrew Goodman, James Earl Chaney, and Michael Schwerner

FBI photographs of Andrew Goodman, James Earl Chaney, and Michael Schwerner

President Johnson signs the Civil Rights Act, the most sweeping civil rights legislation since Reconstruction. It prohibits discrimination of all kinds based on race, color, religion, or national origin (July 2).

The bodies of three civil-rights workers are found. Murdered by the KKK, James E. Chaney, Andrew Goodman, and Michael Schwerner had been working to register black voters in Mississippi (Aug.).

Martin Luther King receives the Nobel Peace Prize. (Oct.)

1965
Malcolm X

Malcolm X, black nationalist and founder of the Organization of Afro-American Unity, is assassinated (Feb. 21).

State troopers violently attack peaceful demonstrators led by Rev. Martin Luther King, Jr., as they try to cross the Pettus Bridge in Selma, Ala. Fifty marchers are hospitalized on "Bloody Sunday," after police use tear gas, whips, and clubs against them. The march is considered the catalyst for pushing through the voting rights act five months later (March 7).

Congress passes the Voting Rights Act of 1965, making it easier for Southern blacks to register to vote. Literacy tests, poll taxes, and other such requirements that were used to restrict black voting are made illegal (Aug. 10).

In six days of rioting in Watts, a black section of Los Angeles, 35 people are killed and 883 injured (Aug. 11-16).

1966
Members of The Black Panthers Party

The Black Panthers are founded by Huey Newton and Bobby Seale (Oct.).

1967
Thurgood Marshall
Supreme Court Justice Thurgood Marshall

Stokely Carmichael, a leader of the Student Nonviolent Coordinating Committee (SNCC), coins the phrase "black power" in a speech in Seattle (April 19).

Major race riots take place in Newark (July 12-16) and Detroit (July 23-30).

President Johnson appoints Thurgood Marshall to the Supreme Court. He becomes the first black Supreme Court Justice.

The Supreme Court rules in Loving v. Virginia that prohibiting interracial marriage is unconstitutional. Sixteen states still have anti-miscegenation laws and are forced to revise them.

1968
Eyewitnesses to the assassination of Martin Luther King, Jr.

Martin Luther King, Jr., is assassinated in Memphis, Tenn. (April 4).

President Johnson signs the Civil Rights Act of 1968, prohibiting discrimination in the sale, rental, and financing of housing (April 11).

1972
The infamous Tuskegee Syphilis experiment ends. Begun in 1932, the U.S. Public Health Service's 40-year experiment on 399 black men in the late stages of syphilis has been described as an experiment that "used human beings as laboratory animals in a long and inefficient study of how long it takes syphilis to kill someone."

1978
The Supreme Court case, Regents of the University of California v. Bakke upheld the constitutionality of affirmative action, but imposed limitations on it to ensure that providing greater opportunities for minorities did not come at the expense of the rights of the majority (June 28).

1992
The first race riots in decades erupt in south-central Los Angeles after a jury acquits four white police officers for the videotaped beating of an African-American Rodney King (April 29).

2003
In Grutter v. Bollinger, the most important affirmative action decision since the 1978 Bakke case, the Supreme Court (5–4) upholds the University of

Michigan Law School's policy, ruling that race can be one of many factors considered by colleges when selecting their students because it furthers "a compelling interest in obtaining the educational benefits that flow from a diverse student body." (June 23)

2006

In Parents v. Seattle and Meredith v. Jefferson, affirmative action suffers a setback when a bitterly divided court rules, 5–4, that programs in Seattle and Louisville, Ky., which tried to maintain diversity in schools by considering race when assigning students to schools, are unconstitutional.

2008

Sen. Barack Obama, Democrat from Chicago, becomes the first African American to be nominated as a major party nominee for president.

On November 4, Barack Obama, became the first African American to be elected president of the United States, defeating Republican candidate, Sen. John McCain.

Think you are smart? Go ahead, give It a try! (Answer key appears at the bottom of the page.)

African-American Quiz I & II

"It's true that Black History has been suppressed or ignored in the telling the story of the history of the world. For decades, almost on a daily basis, Black people fight for the truth to be heard. And many times, the Black community gets exorcised over the fact that their white colleagues, classmates, friends, enemies and associates are ignorant to the contributions and history of the Black race. However, traditional education has not shined the light on Black achievements for ANYONE to see, and for the most part, Blacks are as ignorant to our history as we accuse Whites as being.

Below is an informational quiz for your own pleasure." - Author of comments Unknown

African American History Month Quiz I

1. Who told the Senate Armed Services Committee in 1948 that he would urge black youths to resist the draft unless discrimination was banned?

2. What was the only Southern state to permit slave enlistments in the military in 1780?

3. What was the first Black-owned company to be traded on the New York Stock Exchange?

4. Who was the first African American car manufacturer in 1916?

5. What was the first all-Black religious denomination in the United States?

6. Which European nation was the first to stop trading African slaves to the United States in 1794?

7. Who organized the 1941 exhibition, "Afro-American Art on Both Continents," which included the works of Romare Bearden and the Delaney Brothers?

8. Name the author who wrote The Third Life of Grange Copeland, published in 1970?

9. Who was the three time Super Bowl champion player who returned to his Florida alma mater to receive his bachelor's degree in 1996?

10. Who wrote the script for the 1975 hit, Cooley High?

11. Denzel Washington played in what 1981 Pulitzer Prize-winning play by Charles Fuller?

12. Who was the only other black actress to win the Academy Award's Best Supporting Actress Oscar since Hattie McDaniel in 1939?

13. Who sang Martin Luther King, Jr.'s favorite gospel song, "Precious Lord, Take My Hand," after his funeral procession in 1968?

14. When did James Del Rio become the first African American mortgage banker? 1953? 1976? 1989? 1947?

15. In 1990 the Mystery Writers of America nominated this novel, written by Walter Mosley, as best of the year.

16. By the eighteenth century, what colony was the leader in the slave trade?

17. In what year did Harriet Tubman escape from slavery?

18. Name an African American enterprise that you patronize.

19. During the nineteenth century, how many states had laws prohibiting interracial marriage?

20. Which state east of the Mississippi was the first to give African American women the right to vote, in 1913?

1. A. Philip Randolph
2. Maryland
3. BET Holdings
4. Frederick Douglass Patterson
5. The African Methodist Episcopal Church (AME)
6. France
7. Alain Locke
8. Alice Walker

9. Emmitt Smith
10. Eric Monte
11. A Soldier's Story
12. Whoopi Goldberg
13. Mahalia Jackson
14. 1953
15. Devil in a Blue Dress
16. Rhode Island
17. 1849
18. [You provide]
19. Thirty-eight
20. Illinois

African American History Month Quiz II

1. What was the nickname for the all-Black 332nd Fighter Group of the U.S. Army Air Corps, which escorted Allied bombers through European airspace on 1,578 missions during World War II?

2. Who developed the first major African American-sponsored shopping center, Progress Plaza, in Philadelphia, Pa.

3. The hymn, "Lift Ev'ry Voice and Sing," by James Weldon Johnson, was meant to celebrate whose birthday?

4. A pitcher in the Negro Baseball League for 25 years, developer of the bat-badger, jumpball, and drooper, he was elected to the Baseball Hall of Fame in 1971--name him.

5. Besides being a movie director, composer, author and semi-pro basketball player, he was a photographer for Life magazine from 1948 to 1972.

6. Having worked as an elevator operator for four dollars weekly, he achieved fame upon publication of Lyrics of Lowly Life in 1896.

7. In what year did amateur night at New York's famous Apollo Theater begin?

8. Who holds the record of 100 points scored in a single NBA game?

9. Despite a 1792 discriminatory law against Blacks in the new U.S. military, which of the country's armed forces began to enlist free blacks in the 1790's?

10. What service did the first African American female millionaire, Madame C. J. Walker provide?

11. What tennis champion and golfer earned her place in the Black Hall of Fame in 1974?

12. This graduate of Yale Law School was appointed commissioner and chairman of the U.S. Equal Employment Opportunity Commission by President Ronald Reagan in 1982.

13. In this tribute to 1960's R&B groups, Robert Townsend acted in and directed this movie--name it.

14. Who founded the first major African American national union, the Brotherhood of Sleeping Car Porters?

15. Who won the Ladies World Figure Skating Championship in 1986?

16. Name an African American enterprise that you patronize.

17. A scholar of West Indian dance and culture, she also, originated the role of Georgia Browne in the 1940 Broadway musical, Cabin in the Sky.

18. In what field were 44% of the doctorate degrees awarded in 1995 to African Americans, according to the National Research Council?

19. Who founded the National Negro Business League?

20. At age 76, this former slave and eminent scientist narrated a 1940 documentary dramatizing his struggles and successes to a young boy pondering the options for the future .

ANSWERS TO QUIZ II

1. The Tuskegee Airmen
2. Leon Howard Sullivan
3. Abraham Lincoln
4. Satchel Paige

5. Gordon Parks
6. Paul Lawrence Dunbar
7. 1934
8. Wilt Chamberlin
9. U.S. Navy
10. Hair styling process for African American women
11. Althea Gibson
12. Clarence Thomas
13. The Five Heartbeats
14. A. Philip Randolph
15. Debi Thomas
16. [You provide]
17. Katherine Dunham
18. Education
19. Booker T. Washington
20. George Washington Carver

Americans have recognized black history annually since 1926, first as "Negro History Week" and later as "Black History Month." What you might not know is that black history had barely begun to be studied-or even documented-when the tradition originated. Although blacks have been in America at least as far back as colonial times, it was not until the 20th century that they gained a respectable presence in the history books.

Blacks Absent from History Books

The History of black history

We owe the celebration of Black History Month, and more importantly, the study of black history, to Dr. Carter G. Woodson. Born to parents who were former slaves, he spent his childhood working in the Kentucky coal mines and enrolled in high school at age twenty. He graduated within two years and later went on to earn a Ph.D. from Harvard. The scholar was disturbed to find in his studies that history books largely ignored the black American population-and when blacks did figure into the picture, it was generally in ways that reflected the inferior social position they were assigned at the time.
Established Journal of Negro History

Woodson, always one to act on his ambitions, decided to take on the challenge of writing black Americans into the nation's history. He established the Association for the Study of Negro Life and History (now called the Association for the Study of Afro-American Life and History) in 1915, and a year later founded the widely respected Journal of Negro History. In 1926, he launched Negro History Week as an initiative to bring national attention to the contributions of black people throughout American history.

Woodson chose the second week of February for Negro History Week because it marks the birthdays of two men who greatly influenced the black American population, Frederick Douglass and Abraham Lincoln. However, February has much more than Douglass and Lincoln to show for its significance in black American history. For example:

* February 23, 1868:
    W. E. B. DuBois, important civil rights leader and co-founder of the NAACP, was born.

* February 3, 1870:
    The 15th Amendment was passed, granting blacks the right to vote.

* February 25, 1870:
    The first black U.S. senator, Hiram R. Revels (1822-1901), took his oath of office.

* February 12, 1909:

The National Association for the Advancement of Colored People (NAACP) was founded by a group of concerned black and white citizens in New York City.

* February 1, 1960:

In what would become a civil-rights movement milestone, a group of black Greensboro, N.C., college students began a sit-in at a segregated Woolworth's lunch counter.

* February 21, 1965:

Malcolm X, the militant leader who promoted Black Nationalism, was shot to death by three Black Muslims.

Black Inventor Museum

Welcome to the Black Inventor Museum - a look at the great and often unrecognized leaders in the field of invention and innovation. For more than 300 years, black inventors have served as pioneers in the field of science and have made enormous impacts on society. As African Americans sought freedom and equality, many among them, scientists, educators and even slaves, developed the tools and processes that helped to shape the modern agricultural, industrial and technological landscape. While some are famous, many remain unknown, but their contributions have assured that their stories are not only about black history, but about world history.

Spectrometer : Willard H Bennett and George Edward Alcorn
Willard H Bennett was the inventor of the radio frequency mass spectrometer. George Edward Alcorn invented a method of fabricating an imaging X-ray spectrometer.

Nathaniel Alexander
Nathaniel Alexander patented a folding chair.

Virgie Ammons was an inventor and woman of color who invented a device for dampening fireplaces. Little is known about the life of Virgie Ammons.

Benjamin Banneker (1731-1806)Benjamin Banneker was a self-educated scientist, astronomer, inventor, writer, and antislavery publicist. He built a striking clock entirely from wood, published a Farmers' Almanac, and actively campaigned against slavery. He was one of the first African Americans to gain distinction in science.

Benjamin Banneker was born in 1731 just outside of Baltimore, Maryland, the son of a slave. His grandfather had been a member of a royal family in Africa and was wise in agricultural endeavors. As a young man, Benjamin was allowed to enroll in a school run by Quakers and excelled in his studies, particularly in mathematics. Soon, he had progressed beyond the capabilities of his teacher and would often make up his own math problems in order to solve them.

Patricia Bath

Patricia Bath became the first African American woman doctor to receive a patent for a medical invention.

Dr. Patricia Bath, an ophthalmologist from New York, but living in Los Angeles when she received her patent, became the first African American woman doctor to receive a patent for a medical invention. Patricia Bath's patent (no. 4,744,360), a method for removing cataract lenses, transformed eye surgery, using a laser device making the procedure more accurate. **When Patricia Era Bath was born on November 4, 1942**, she could have succumbed to the pressures and stresses associated with growing up in Harlem, New York. With the uncertainty present because of World War II and the challenges for members of Black communities in the 1940's, one might little expect that a top flight scientist would emerge from their midst. Patricia Bath, however, saw only excitement and opportunity in her future, sentiments instilled by her parents. Her father, Rupert, was well-educated and an eclectic spirit. He was the first Black motorman for the New York City subway system, served as a merchant seaman, traveling abroad and wrote a newspaper column. Her mother Gladys was the descendant of African slaves and Cherokee Native Americans. She worked as a housewife and domestic, saving money for her children's education. Rupert was able to tell his daughter stories about his travels around the world, deepening her curiosity about people in other countries and their struggles. Her mother encouraged her to read constantly and broadened Patricia's interest in science by buying her a chemistry set. With the direction and encouragement offered by her parents, Patricia quickly proved worthy of their efforts. In 1981 she began work on her most well-known invention which she would call a "Laserphaco Probe." The device employed a laser as well as two tubes, one for irrigation and one for aspiration (suction). The laser would be used to make a small incision in the eye and the laser energy would vaporize the cataracts within a couple of minutes. The damaged lens would then be flushed with liquids and then gently extracted by the suction tube. With the liquids still being washed into the eye, a new lens could be easily inserted. Additionally, this procedure could be used for initial cataract surgery and could eliminate much of the discomfort expected, while increasing the accuracy of the surgery. Unfortunately, though her concept was sound, she was unable to find any lasers within the United States that could be adapted for the procedure (the majority of laser technology in the United States was dedicated to military purposes). She was able to find the laser probe she needed in Berlin, Germany and successfully tested the device which she described as an "apparatus for ablating and removing cataract lenses" and later dubbed it the "Laserphaco Probe." Bath sought patent protection for her device and received patents in several countries around the world. She intends to use the proceeds of her patent licenses to benefit the AIPB.

Andrew Beard (1849-1921)
Andrew Beard was a farmer, carpenter, blacksmith, a railroad worker, a businessman and finally an inventor.

Andrew Beard was born a slave on a plantation in Woodland, Alabama, shortly before slavery ended. Andrew Beard was a farmer, carpenter, blacksmith, a railroad worker, a businessman and finally an inventor.

In 1881, he patented his first invention, a plow, and sold the patent rights for $4,000 in 1884. In 1887, Andrew Beard patented a second plow and sold it for $5,200. Beard invested the money he made from his plow inventions into a profitable real-estate business.

Andrew Jackson Beard hailed from Eastlake, Alabama, a small town outside of Birmingham. With the emergence of the railroad industry and its rapid expansion throughout the country, an alarming number of rail men suffered serious injuries to their arms and legs when they were crushed during manual style coupling of railroad cars. During manual coupling, a worker would have to attempt to precisely time the moment when two railroad cars being pushed together would be close enough for that worker to drop a metal pin between their connectors, thus engaging the cars. If the worker was off by one second he might severely damage his arm or leg - many in fact had to undergo amputation.

On November 27, 1897 Beard received a patent for a device he called the Jenny Coupler. The Jenny Coupler automatically joined cars by simply allowing them to bump into each other, or as Beard described it the "horizontal jaws engage each other to connect the cars." Beard sold the rights to his invention for $50,000.00 and the railroad industry was revolutionized.

During his lifetime, Beard received a number of other patents, including a steam driven rotary engine, and a double plow.

Miriam Benjamin

Miriam E. Benjamin was a school teacher living in Washington D.C. In 1888, Ms. Benjamin received a patent for an invention she called a Gong and Signal Chair for Hotels. Her chair, as she stated in her patent application would "reduce the expenses of hotels by decreasing the number of waiters and attendants, to add to the convenience and comfort of guests and to obviate the necessity of hand clapping or calling aloud to obtain the services of pages."

The system worked by pressing a small button on the back of a chair which would relay a signal to a waiting attendant. At the same time a light would illuminate on the chair allowing the attendant to see which guest was in need of assistance. The system was adopted and installed within the United States House of Representatives and was the predecessor of the methods used today on airplanes to signal stewardesses.

Ms. Benjamin was the second Black woman to receive a patent.

Henry Blair was the second Black inventor issued a patent by the United States Patent Office. His first invention was a seed planter which enabled farmers to plant more corn utilizing less labor in a smaller period of time. Two years later, in 1836, Blair received a second patent for a corn harvester. Blair had been a successful farmer for years and developed the inventions as a means of increasing efficiency in farming.

It is noteworthy that in both of his patents he was listed as a "colored man", the only example of an inventor's race being listed or acknowledged on an issued patent.

Sarah Boone received a patent on April 26, 1892 for a device which would help to neatly iron clothing. This device, the predecessor to our modern ironing board was made of a narrow wooden board, with collapsible legs and a padded cover and was specifically designed for the fitted clothing worn during that time period.

Prior to her inventions, people were forced to resort to simply using a table or being creative in laying a plank of wood across two chairs or small tables.

Otis F. Boykin was born on August 29, 1920 in Dallas, Texas. After graduating high school, he attended Fisk College in Nashville, Tennessee. He graduated in 1941 and took a job as a laboratory assistant with the Majestic Radio and TV Corporation in Chicago, Illinois. He undertook various tasks but excelled at testing automatic aircraft controls, ultimately serving as a supervisor. Three years later he left Majestic and took a position as a research engineer with the P.J. Nielsen Research Laboratories. Soon thereafter, he decided to try to develop a business of his own a founded Boykin-Fruth, Incorporated. At the same time, he decided to continue his education, pursuing graduate studies at the Illinois Institute of Technology in Chicago, Illinois. He attended classes in 1946 and 1947 but was forced to drop out because he lacked the funds to pay the next year's tuition.

Despite this setback, Boykin realized that a Masters Degree was not a pre-requisite for inventive competence. He set out to work on project that he had contemplated while in school. At the time, the field of electronics was very popular among the science community and Boykin took a special interest in working with resistors. A resistor is an electronic component that slows the flow of an electrical current. This is necessary to prevent too much electricity from passing through a component than is necessary or even safe. Boykin sought and received a patent for a wire precision resistor on June 16, 1959. This resistor allowed for specific amounts of current to flow through for a specific purpose and would be used in radios and televisions. Two years later, he created another resistor that could be manufactured very inexpensively. It was a breakthrough device as it could withstand extreme changes in temperature and tolerate and withstand various levels of pressure and physical trauma without impairing its effectiveness. The chip was cheaper and more reliable than others on the market. Not surprisingly, it was in great demand as he received orders from consumer electronics manufacturers, the United States military and electronics behemoth IBM.

In 1964, Boykin moved to Paris, creating electronic innovations for a new market of customers. Most of these creations involved electrical resistance components (including small component thick-film resistors used in computers and variable resistors used in guided missile systems) but he also created other important products including a chemical air filter and a burglarproof cash register. His most famous invention, however, was a control unit for the pacemaker, which used electrical impulses to stimulate the heart and create a steady heartbeat. In a tragic irony, Boykin died in 1982 as a result of heart failure.

Otis Boykin proved that the setback of having to drop out of school was not enough to deter him from his dream of becoming an inventor and having a long-lasting effect on the world.

Benjamin Bradley was born around 1830 as a slave in Maryland. He was able to read and write, although at the time it was illegal for a slave to do so (he likely learned from the Master's children). He was put to work in a printing office and at the age of 16 began working with scrap he found, modeling it into a small ship. Eventually, with an intuitiveness that seemed far beyond him, he improved on his creation until he had built a working steam engine, made from a piece of a gun-barrel, pewter, pieces of round steel and some nearby junk. Those around him were so astounded by his high level of intelligence that he was placed in a new job, this time at the United States Naval Academy in Annapolis, Maryland.

Despite enjoying his job with the Naval Academy, Bradley had not forgotten his steam engine creation. He used the money he had been able to save from his job as well as the proceeds of the sale of his original engine (to a Naval Academy student) to build a larger model. Eventually he was able to finish an engine large enough to drive the first steam-powered warship at 16 knots. At the time, because he was a slave, he was unable to secure a patent for his engine. His Master Aster did, however, allow him to sell the engine and he used that money to purchase his freedom.

C. B. Brooks designed the street sweeper and patented it on March 17, 1896. Prior to his invention, streets were cleaned manually by workers picking up trash by hand or sweeping it with brooms. Brooks' invention was made of a truck with a series of broom-like brushes attached which pushed trash and debris off onto the side of the road.

The street sweeper initially faced a lot of resentment from workers who felt they could do a better job. Eventually, as cities grew bigger and more and more litter accumulated, the street sweeper became indispensable.

Henry Brown was an inventor who saw a need for a convenient and secure way to store money, valuables and important papers. At that time, people commonly kept those type of items in wooden or cardboard boxes in their homes or entrusted them to local banks. Both of these options presented dilemmas While banks generally provided safety against theft, they did not prevent bank employees from reading through personal papers. At the same time, keeping the items at home could help to keep prying eyes away, but there was little to prevent burglars from quickly and easily grabbing valuables and making off with them.

Brown decided to create a safer container and developed a forged-metal container which could be sealed with a lock and key. He patented his **receptacle for storing and preserving papers** on November 2, 1886 and it developed into what is now known as a strongbox.

George Carruthers was born on October 1, 1939 in Cincinnati, Ohio. His father was a civil engineer while his mother was a homemaker. The family lived in Milford, Ohio and George was an avid science fiction reader and constructed model rockets with help and encouragement from his father. He also had an interest in astronomy, and at age 10, built his first telescope with a cardboard tube and a lens he purchased through mail-order. When his father passed away suddenly, the family moved to his mother's hometown of Chicago, Illinois. There George spent a lot of time in the Chicago libraries and museums and in the Adler Planetarium He joined various science clubs and was a member of the Chicago Rocket Society. He read with particular interest about the space exploits of the Naval Research Laboratory in Washington, DC and upon graduating from Englewood High School in 1957 he enrolled in the University of Illinois.

Carruthers stayed at the University of Illinois for seven years, receiving a Bachelor of Science degree in Aeronautical Engineering in 1961, a Master's degree in Nuclear Engineering in 1962 and a Ph.D. in Aeronautical and Astronomical Engineering in 1964 (his thesis focused on atomic nitrogen recombination). In his own words, "[W]hen I was in college, I was undecided whether to pursue aerospace engineering or astronomy as my major, so I decided to take courses in both of them." While doing his graduate work, he also worked as a research and teaching assistant, working with plasma and gases. Upon finishing his Ph.D., he immediately accepted a position with the Naval Research Laboratory (NRL) as a Research Physicist in 1964, having received a fellowship in Rocket Astronomy from the National Science Foundation.

Upon joining the NRL, Carruthers focused his attention on far ultraviolet astronomy, observing the Earth's upper atmosphere and other astronomical phenomena. In 1966, he became a research assistant at the NRL's E.O. Hulburt Center for Space Research where he began research on ways to create visual images as a means for understanding the physical elements of deep space. He particularly focused on creating a device to analyze and illuminate ultraviolet radiation. His belief was "[T]he far ultraviolet... is of great importance to the astronomer because it allows the detection and measurements of common elements (hydrogen, oxygen, nitrogen, carbon, and many others) in their cool, unexcited state... This allows more accurate measurements of the compositions of interstellar gas, planetary atmospheres, etc. The ultraviolet also conveys important information on solid particles in interstellar space... and provides for much more accurate measurements of the energy output of very hot stars…". In 1969, Carruthers received a patent for his invention the "Image Converter for Detecting Electromagnetic Radiation Especially in Short Wave Lengths" which detected electromagnetic radiation in short wave lengths.

Further extending his research, he was the principle inventor of the Far Ultraviolet Camera/Spectrograph which would ultimately be used on the Apollo 16 mission to the moon. Ultraviolet (UV) light is the range of electromagnetic radiation that lies between visible light and X-Rays. UV light, thus allows us to take readings of and understand objects and elements in space that are unrecognizable to the naked eye. The 50 lbs., gold-plated camera system was able to record radiation existing in the upper half of the ultraviolet system of the atmosphere. The camera allowed views of stars and celestial bodies and looks into the solar system thousands of miles away, as well as of the Earth. A second version of the camera was sent on the 1974 Sky Lab space flight to study comets (it would be used to observe Halley's, West's and Kohoutek's comets). One of the great uses of the camera was to permit a viewer to visually see the effects of pollution on the atmosphere. The camera also was able, for the first time, to detect hydrogen in space, which gave an indication that plants were not the only source of oxygen for the Earth and led to a renewed debate about the origin of stars.

George Carruthers has continued to offer innovation in the areas of astronomy and physics and has been active in outreach programs seeking to bring science to youth around the country. He has been lauded for his efforts and achievements. He was named Black Engineer of the Year in 1987, awarded the Arthur Fleming Award in 1971, the Exceptional Achievement Scientific Award from NASA in 1972, the Warner Prize in 1973 and was inducted into National Inventors Hall of Fame in 2003. His success is primed to lead to greater achievements by those who follow in his footsteps in the future.

George Washington Carver was born in 1860 in Diamond Grove, Missouri and despite early difficulties would rise to become one of the most celebrated and respected scientists in United States history. His important discoveries and methods enabled farmers through the south and mid west to become profitable and prosperous.

George was born the sickly child of two slaves and would remain frail for most of his childhood. One night a band of raiders attacked his family and stole George and his mother. Days later, George was found unharmed by neighbors and was traded back to his owners in exchange for a racehorse. Because of his frailty, George was not suited for work in the fields but he did possess a great interest in plants and was very eager to learn more about them.

His master sent him to Neosho, Missouri for an early education and he graduated from Minneapolis High School in Kansas. He eventually mailed an application to Highland University in Kansas and was not only accepted but also offered a scholarship. Happily, George traveled to the school to accept the scholarship but upon meeting George, the University president asked "why didn't you tell me you were a Negro?" and promptly withdrew the scholarship and the acceptance.

In 1887 Carver was accepted into Simpson College in Indianola, Iowa where he became well respected for his artistic talent (in later days his art would be included in the spectacular World's Columbian Exposition Art Exhibit.) Carver's interests, however, lay more in science and he transferred from Simpson to Iowa Agricultural College (which is now known as Iowa State University.) He distinguished himself so much that upon graduation he was offered a position on the school's faculty, the first Black accorded the honor. Carver was allowed great freedom in working in agriculture and botany in the University's greenhouses. In 1895, Carver co-authored a series of papers on the prevention and cures for fungus diseases affecting cherry plants.

In 1896 he received his Master's degree in agriculture and in 1897 discovered two fungi that would be named after him. At this point, the most pivotal moment of his life arose - he was summoned by Booker T. Washington to teach at Tuskegee Normal and Industrial Institute. He was appointed director of agriculture and quickly set out to completely correct its wretched state. He was given a 20 acre shabby piece of land and along with his students planted peas on it. Like all <u>legumes</u>, the peas had nitrogen-fixing bacteria on their roots which took nitrogen from the air and converted it into nitrates which then worked to fertilize the soil. The depleted soil quickly became rich and fertile, so much so that he was able to grow 500 pounds of cotton on each acre of land he worked on.

Carver soon instructed nearby farmers on his methods of improving the soil and taught them how to rotate their crops to promote a better quality of soil. Most of the staple crops of the south (tobacco and cotton) stole nutrients from the soil, but these nutrients could be returned to the soil by planting legumes. Thus, in order to improve the soil, Carver instructed the farmers to plant peanuts, which could be harvested easily and fed to livestock. The farmers were ecstatic with the tremendous quality of cotton and tobacco they grew later but quickly grew angry because the amount of peanuts they harvested was too plentiful and began to rot in overflowing warehouses. Within a week, Carver had experimented and devised dozens of uses for the peanut, including milk and cheese. In later years he would produce more than 300 products that could be developed from the lowly peanut, including ink, facial cream, shampoo and soap.

Suddenly, the same farmers who cursed him now found that a new industry had sprung up that could use their surplus peanuts. Next, Carver looked at ways of utilizing the sweet potato and was able to develop more than 115 products from it including flour, starch and synthetic rubber (the United States Army utilized many of his products during World War I).

Carver did not stop with these discoveries. From the inexpensive pecan he developed more than 75 products, from discarded corn stalks dozens of uses and from common clays he created dyes and paints. Suddenly Carver's fame grew and grew until he was invited to speak before the United States Congress and was consulted by titans of industry and invention. Henry Ford, head of Ford Motor Company invited Carver to his Dearborn, Michigan plant where the two devised a way to use goldenrod, a plant weed, to create synthetic rubber. Thomas Edison, the great inventor was so enthusiastic about him that he asked Carver to move to Orange Grove, New Jersey to work at the Edison Laboratories at an annual salary of $100,000 per year and state of the art facilities. He declined the generous offer, wanting to continue on at Tuskegee.

He was elected a Fellow of the Royal Society of Arts, Manufacturers and Commerce of Britain in 1916, awarded the Spingarn Medal from the National Association for the Advancement of Colored People in 1923, and in 1939 was awarded the Theodore Roosevelt Medal for "distinguished research in agricultural chemistry." He was appointed to various boards and committees by the United States Department of Agriculture and was named Man of the Year in 1940 by the International Federation of Architects, Engineers, Chemists and Technicians. Finally, he received honorary Doctor of Science degrees from Simpson College as well as the University of Rochester.

George Washington Carver died on January 5, 1943 on the campus of Tuskegee Institute. He was honored by various levels of State and Federal Government as well as by foreign leaders worldwide. The United States government designated the farmland upon which he grew up as a national monument and January 5, 1946 was honored as George Washington Carver day. He was truly a pioneer in his field and has become one of the few Black inventors recognized by mainstream America.

M. A. Cherry developed two devices that would one day evolve into very useful items for transportation. The first device was called a velocipede and consisted of a metal frame upon which were attached two or three wheels. Someone sitting on the seat of the apparatus could propel themselves forward at considerable speeds by moving their feet along the ground in a fast walking or running motion. Cherry's model, which he patented on May 8, 1888, greatly improved upon other similar devices and has evolved into what are now known as the bicycle and the tricycle.

Seven years later, Cherry set out to solve a problem with streetcars. Whenever the front of a streetcar accidentally collided with another object, the streetcar was severely damaged, often having to be totally replaced. Cherry patented the street car fender on January 1, 1895 and added safety for passengers and employees. The fender, which was a piece of metal attached to the front of the streetcar, acted as a shock absorber, thereby diminishing the force of the impact in the event of an accident. This device has been modified through the years and is now used on most transportation devices.

David Crosthwait was born in Nashville, Tennessee and moved to Kansas City, Missouri where he attended high school. He went on to attend Purdue University where he obtained a Bachelor of Science degree in 1913 and a Master of Engineering degree in 1920.

In 1913 Crosthwait moved to Marshalltown, Iowa where he began working for the Durham Company, designing heating installations. In 1925 he was named the director of the research department, overseeing a staff of engineers and chemists. His research concerned heating and ventilating and in the coming years he obtained 39 patents for various devices including heating systems, vacuum pumps, refrigeration methods and processes and temperature regulating devices. His most famous creation was the heating system for New York's famous Radio City Music Hall.

George Crum was the head chef at the Cary Moon's Lake House in Lake Saratoga, New York when he set out to prepare the evening dinner for the guests. He intended to make french fries but sliced the potatoes too thinly. After deep frying them he found them very thin and very crisp. The hungry guests did not seem to mind and George began preparing the potatoes this way and they would soon become known as potato chips.

While George Crum's creation came about accidentally, the potato chip industry produces billions of dollars in sales each year.

Born in Jefferson City, Tennessee on March 2, 1957, Mark Dean found that success ran in his bloodlines. His grandfather was a high school principal and his father worked as a supervisor for the Tennessee Valley Authority Dam. A bright and energetic child, he often endured questions from grade school classmates, asking if he was really Black because Black people were not supposed to be that smart. Mark was an outstanding high school athlete as well as a straight A student. His success continued in college as he graduated at the top of his class with a Bachelor of Science in Electrical Engineering from the University of Tennessee in 1979.

In 1980, Dean was invited to join IBM as an engineer. Despite his new position, he continued his education and received a Master's Degree in Electrical Engineering from Florida Atlantic University in 1982. In his capacity as an engineer for IBM, he didn't take long to make a big impact, serving as the chief engineer for the team that developed the IBM PC/AT, the original home/office computer. Along with his colleague Dennis Moeller, he developed the Industry Standard Architecture (ISA) systems bus, a component that allowed multiple peripheral devices such as a modems and printers to be connected to a PC, thus making the PC a practical and affordable component of the home or small business office. Dean would own three of the original nine patents that all PCs are based upon. Dean followed up with PS/2 Models 70 or 80, and the Color Graphics Adapter (which allowed for color display on the PC).

Despite his enormous success, Dean realized that there was more to learn and more than he could achieve, so he entered Stanford University and in 1992 received a Ph.D. in Electrical Engineering. Five years later he was named as the director of the Austin Research Laboratory and director of Advanced Technology Development for the IBM Enterprise Server Group. Under his leadership, in 1999 his team made several significant breakthroughs including the testing of the first gigahertz CMOS microprocessor. With this great success he was named the vice president for Systems Research at IBM's Watson Research Center in Yorktown Heights, New York, then as a vice president in IBM's Storage Technology Group, focused on the company's storage systems strategy and technology roadmap. He was later named vice president for hardware and systems architecture in IBM's Systems and Technology Group (STG) in Tucson, Arizona and finally the vice president of the IBM Almaden Research Center in San Jose, California.

In addition to the prestigious titles with their inherent responsibilities, Dr. Dean was named an IBM fellow, the highest technical honor awarded by the company (only 50 of IBM's 310,000 employees are IBM Fellows and he was the first Black person so honored). In 1997, along with his friend Dennis Moeller, he was inducted into the National Inventors Hall of Fame (with Hall membership at around 150) and in 2001 was elected a member of the National Academy of Engineers. With more than 40 patents or patents pending, Dr. Dean is poised to continue his far reaching impact on the world of science and the home and workplace.

Joseph Dickinson was born in Canada in 1955 and moved to Michigan in 1870. He learned about various types of organs while working for the Clough and Warren Organ Company in Detroit in 1872. One of the organs he designed was awarded a prize at the Centennial Exposition in Philadelphia, Pennsylvania in 1876 and Dickinson was quickly hired to build organs for major customers, including the Royal Family of Portugal.

After marrying Eva Gould in 1884, Dickinson formed the Dickinson-Gould Organ Company along with his father-in-law. The company manufactured reed organs and Dickinson received numerous patents for them, the last coming in 1912.

In 1891, anyone interested in mailing a letter would have to make the long trip o the post office. P. B. Downing designed a metal box with four legs which he patented on October 27, 1891. He called his device a street letter box and it is the predecessor of today's mailbox.

One year earlier, Downing patented an electrical switch for railroads which allowed railroad workers to supply or shut off power to trains at appropriate times. Based on this design, innovators would later create electrical switches such as light switches used in the home.

Charles Drew was born on June 3, 1904 in Washington, D.C., the son of Richard and Nora Drew and eldest of five children. Charles was one of those rare individuals who seemed to excel at everything he did and on every level and would go on to become of pioneer in the field of medicine.

Charles' early interests were in education, particularly in medicine, but he was also an outstanding athlete. As a youngster he was an award winning swimmer and starred at Dunbar High School in football, baseball, basketball and track and field, winning the James E. Walker Memorial medal as his school's best all around athlete. After graduation from Dunbar in 1922, he went on to attend Amherst College in Massachusetts where he captained the track team and starred as a halfback on the school's football team, winning the Thomas W. Ashley Memorial trophy in his junior year as the team most valuable player and being named to the All-American team. Upon graduation from Amherst in 1926 he was awarded the Howard Hill Mossman trophy as the man who contributed the most to Amherst athletics during his four years in school.

After graduation from Amherst, Drew took on a position as a biology teacher at Morgan State University in Baltimore, Maryland and also served as the school's Athletic Director. During his two years at Morgan State, he helped to turn the school's basketball and football programs into collegiate champions.

In 1928, Charles decided to pursue his interest in medicine and enrolled at McGill University in Montreal, Canada. He was received as a member of the Medical Honorary Society and graduated in 1933 with Master of Surgery and Doctor of Medicine degrees, finishing second in his class of 127 students. He stayed in Montreal for a while as an intern at Montreal General Hospital and at the Royal Victoria Hospital. In 1935, he returned to the United States and began working as an instructor of pathology at Howard University in Washington, D.C. He was also a resident at Freedmen's Hospital (the teaching hospital for Howard University) and was awarded the Rockefeller Foundation Research Fellowship. He spent two years at Columbia University in New York attending classes and working as a resident at the Columbia University Presbyterian Hospital. During this time he became involved in research on blood and blood transfusions.

Years back, while a student at McGill, he had saved a man by giving him a blood transfusion and had studied under Dr. John Beattie, an instructor of anatomy who was intensely interested in blood transfusions. Now at Columbia, he wrote a dissertation on "Banked Blood" in which he described a technique he developed for the long-term preservation of blood plasma. Prior to his discovery, blood could not be stored for more than two days because of the rapid breakdown of red blood cells. Drew had discovered that by separating the plasma (the liquid part of blood) from the whole blood (in which the red blood cells exist) and then refrigerating them separately, they could be combined up to a week later for a blood transfusion. He also discovered that while everyone has a certain type of blood (A, B, AB, or O) and thus are prevented from receiving a full blood transfusion from someone with different blood, everyone has the same type of plasma. Thus, in certain cases where a whole blood transfusion is not necessary, it was sufficient to give a plasma transfusion which could be administered to anyone, regardless of their blood type. He convinced Columbia University to establish a blood bank and soon was asked to go to England to help set up that country's first blood bank. Drew became the first Black to receive a Doctor of Medical Science degree from Columbia and was now gaining a reputation worldwide.

On September 29, 1939, Charles married Lenore Robbins, with whom he would have four children. At the same time, however, World War II was breaking out in Europe. Drew was named the Supervisor of the Blood Transfusion Association for New York City and oversaw its efforts towards providing plasma to the British Blood Bank. He was later named a project director for the American Red Cross but soon resigned his post after the United States War Department issued a directive that blood taken from White donors should be segregated from that of Black donors.

In 1942, Drew returned to Howard University to head its Department of Surgery, as well as the Chief of Surgery at Freedmen's Hospital. Later he was named Chief of Staff and Medical Director for the Hospital. In 1948 he was awarded the Spingarn Medal from the National Association for the Advancement of Colored People for his work on blood plasma. He was also presented with the E. S. Jones Award for Research in Medical Science and became the first Black to be appointed an examiner by the American Board of Surgery. In 1945 he was presented honorary degrees of Doctor of Science from Virginia State College as well as Amherst College where he attended as an undergraduate student. In 1946 he was elected Fellow of the International College of Surgeons and in 1949 appointed Surgical Consultant for the United States Army's European Theater of Operations.

Charles Drew died on April 1, 1950 when the automobile he was driving went out of control and turned over. Drew suffered extensive and massive injuries but contrary to popular legend was not denied a blood transfusion by an all-White hospital - he indeed received a transfusion but was beyond the help of the experienced physicians attending to him. His family later wrote letters to those physicians thanking them for the care they provided. Over the years, Drew has been considered one of the most honored and respected figures in the medical field and his development of the blood plasma bank has given a second chance of life to millions.

T. Elkins designed a device that helped with the task of preserving perishable foods by way of refrigeration. At the time, the common way of accomplishing this was by placing items in a large container and surrounding them with large blocks of ice. Unfortunately, the ice generally melted very quickly and the food soon perished.

Elkins' device utilized metal cooling coils which became very cold and would cool down items which they surrounded. The coils were enclosed within a container and perishable items were placed inside. The coils cooled the container to temperature significantly lower than that inside of a room thereby keeping the perishable items cool and fresh for longer periods of time.

Elkins patented this refrigerated apparatus on November 4, 1879 and had previously patented a chamber commode in 1872 and a dining, ironing table and quilting frame combined in 1870.

The early life of Philip Emeagwali seemed destined for poverty in his native land of Nigeria. He was the oldest of nine children and his father, who worked as a nurse's aide, earned only a modest income. As a result, at age 14, Philip was forced to drop out of school in Onitsha. Because he had shown such great promise in mathematics, his father encouraged him to continue learning at home. Every evening, Philip's father would quiz him in math as well as other subjects. He would ask these questions in a rapid-fire manner, prompting Philip to think quickly on his feet. Eventually, Philip was tasked to answer 100 questions in an hour, which to his father's delight, he succeeded in. Unable to attend school, Philip instead journeyed to the public library, spending most of his day there. He sped through books appropriate for his age and moved up to college-level material, studying mathematics, chemistry, physics and English. After a period of study, he applied to take the General Certificate of Education exam (a high-school equivalency exam) through the University of London and he passed it easily.

Having achieved this success, he decided to apply to colleges in Europe and the United States and at age 17 was offered a scholarship by Oregon

State University in the United States. He began his studies at Oregon State in 1974 and received a Bachelor Degree in Mathematics in 1977. He then moved to the Washington, D.C. area and received a Master's Degree in Environmental Engineering from George Washington University in 1981 and a second Master's Degree in Applied Mathematics from the University of Maryland in 1986. During the same period of time he received another Master's Degree from George Washington University, this time in Ocean, Coastal and Marine Engineering. He worked for a period of time as a civil engineer in Maryland and Wyoming, but his real success was yet to come.

In 1987, the Emeagwali was accepted into the University of Michigan's Civil Engineering doctoral program and received a doctoral fellowship. At the time, in the United States, the government and many in academia contended that there were 20 Grand Challenges that faced the world in the areas of science and engineering. One of these challenges was petroleum reservoir simulation. In the petroleum industry, oil is generally found within underground rocks in reservoirs. The oil is extracted by drilling down into the rock and extracting the oil but because of the uncertainties of locating the pocket of oil, industry experts could only confidently hope to extract 10 percent of the oil within a known reservoir and that was done by utilizing supercomputers (which could cost upwards of $30 million) to simulate oil fields and anticipate the flow of the oil therein. In order to extract the oil, water or gas must be pumped into the field to force it upwards. Unfortunately, if done incorrectly, the oil could be forced into an inaccessible pocket and the natural oil flow could be interrupted, thus forcing the oil company to commence drilling again, at considerable expense. Emeagwali, having grown up in Nigeria which boasted grand oil reservoirs., understood that at the time, with oil selling for $20.00 per barrel, just a one percent increase in production from a 20 billion barrel field would result in another $400 million yield, a staggering amount. As part of his doctoral dissertation, he decided to take on the challenge.

Emeagwali had read a 1922 science fiction article written by Lewis Fry Richardson entitled "Weather prediction by numerical processes" which suggested using 64,000 mathematicians do weather forecasting for the entire planet. Based on this article and on the work of German mathematician Paul Fillunger and Russian mathematician B. K. Risenkampf (in partial differential equations), Emeagwali determined that rather than using a supercomputer that used 8 processors, he would instead use 65,536 microprocessors (a microprocessor is basically what is found in desktop computers) to work the necessary computations. He based his decision on an old premise that a large number of chickens, if coordinated in strength and efficiency, will be able to do a better job than a small number of oxen. Thus, his 65,536 microprocessors would work together as chickens and theorized that they could outwork the eight processor (eight oxen) supercomputer. He originally theorized that the 64,000 processors could be used instead of mathematicians to predict the Earth' weather, but then decided to turn his theory towards the petroleum reservoir simulation. The obvious problem was how to gain access to that many computers and how to connect them. Instead he turned to the Connection Machine, a device developed by a company called Thinking Machines. The machine was designed such that it could contain within it up to 65,536 microprocessors interconnected, each with its own RAM and each processing one bit at a time. Emeagwali found that there was a Connection Machine at the Los Alamos National Laboratory (NANL) in New Mexico. Scientists were having a difficult time programming the computer to simulate nuclear blasts and it sat unused for much of the time. He submitted an application and NANL approved his use of their Connection Machine which he accessed remotely through the Internet from Michigan. After setting the parameters, Emeagwali ran his program and was astounded when the machine was able to perform 3.1 billion calculations per second. The program had also determined the amount of oil in the simulated reservoir, the direction of flow and the speed at which it was flowing at each point. The impact of his experiment was immense. By discovering a practical application for utilizing supercomputers, he opened up a whole new market for them. Just seven years later it was estimated that 10 percent of massively parable computers had been purchased by the petroleum industry. Furthermore, it provided the theory of connecting computer around the world to provide a scalable, network through which to share and process information. Using this concept in conjunction with the existing internet backbone, the World Wide Web would emerge as an new entity for providing communications and enhancing commerce. In 1989, in acknowledgement of his discovery, Emeagwali was awarded the Institute of Electrical and Electronics Engineers (IEEE) Gordon Bell Prize which recognizes outstanding achievement in high-performance computing applications.

Encouraged by his success and newly found status, Emeagwali moved forward with further research and provided new theories and concepts for computer design. Many of these were based on the idea that computers were simply an extension of the function of nature and thus that they should be designed based on nature. One of his theories is aimed at exploring long-term effects of greenhouse gases and global warming. Emeagwali offered a new design for a computer based on honeycombs. Based on the theory of tessellated models, Emeagwali broke the Earth's atmosphere into sections that resembled honeycombs created by bees. He reasoned that bees are able to use the most efficient methods to develop their honeycombs and that following principles of honeycomb design in a computer will allow it to work in an optimal fashion. He believes that his hyper ball computer will allow for weather forecasting far into the future and for simulated global warming trends in order to address the problem.

In addition to the aforementioned concept, Emeagwali have created hundreds more. He has lectured around the world and been lauded by for his achievements. He was named the Pioneer of the Year by the National Society of Black Engineers, as well as Scientist of the Year in 1991, the Computer Scientist of the Year by America's National Technical Association in 1993 along with dozens of other tributes.

For someone who was born with little, Philip Emeagwali was able to achieve a lot and has served as an inspiration to millions of people, especially in Nigeria. Former United States President Bill Clinton summed up worldwide sentiment by declaring Emeagwali "One of the great minds of the Information Age."

In 1890, H. Faulkner decided to work on a problem that caused suffering in people everyday - foot problems caused by lack of ventilation inside of shoes. For years people constantly complained about blisters and sores on their feet as well as excessive sweating and aching caused by walking and standing with shoes on which offered no cooling air to circulate within. Faulkner devised a method for placing holes in specific locations within the shoe, thus allowing for adequate circulation and greater comfort.

Faulkner patented the **ventilated shoe** on April 29, 1890 and thereby helped to provide comfort and healthy feet to the world.

D. A. Fisher responded to the needs of furniture workers by trying to make their work easier, safer and more productive. He created and patented two devices which eased the burden of these workers and improved their efforts.

His first invention was aimed at freeing up time for carpenters and furniture makers. At the time, when furniture was being put together, a worker was forced to work in slow steps, pausing at various times to combine pieces of wood together in order to allow glue to bind them. Fisher solved this delay by developing the joiner's clamp, which he patented on April 20, 1875. The joiner's clamp consisted of two pieces of wood connected by two screws. When tightened, the screws pushed the pieces of wood together. He used this device to hold together furniture parts as they were glued, thus freeing the worker to continuing assembling the item. By using applied, balanced pressure, the joiner's clamp caused the wood to bind together, faster and stronger than was previously possible.

Another dilemma facing workers in the furniture industry was the laborious task of moving heavy pieces of furniture. In addition to having to concern themselves with their own physical safety, they also had to worry about dropping the furniture and damaging other items in the room by bumping into them. On March 14, 1876, Fisher patented the furniture caster. This device was a free turning wheel that could (when combined with a few others) allow heavy items to move around a room on rollers, safely and efficiently. This enabled one person to move large pieces of furniture, allowing other workers to tend to other items. This device is now used in almost every industry as well as in most homes.

James Forten was born in 1766 as a free Black man in Philadelphia, Pennsylvania. Over the course of his lifetime, he would make an impact upon the fortunes of industries and the lives of his fellow man.

Forten was the son of Thomas and Sarah Forten and the grandson of slaves. He was raised in Philadelphia and educated in Anthony Benezet's Quaker school for colored children. At age eight, James began working for Robert Bridges sail loft, and worked alongside his father. A year later his father died in a boating accident and James was forced to take on additional work to provide for his family.

When he turned 14 he worked as a powder boy during the Revolutionary War on the Royal Lewis sailing ship. After being captured by the British, he was released and returned home to again begin working in Mr. Bridges loft. Pleased with his work and ambition, Mr. Bridges eventually appointed him to the foreman's position in the loft. In 1798 Bridges decided to retire and wanted Forten to remain in charge of the loft. He loaned enough money to Forten to purchase the loft and soon James owned the business, employing 38 people.

Around this time, Forten began experimenting with different types of sails for ships and finally invented one that he found was better suited for maneuvering and maintaining greater speeds. Although he did not patent the sail, he was able to benefit financially, as his sailing loft became one of the most successful and prosperous ones in Philadelphia.

The fortune he soon made was enormous for any man, Black or White. Forten spent his money and lived a luxurious life, but he also made good use of his resources on people other than his self. More than half of his considerable fortune was devoted towards abolitionist causes. He often purchased slaves freedom, helped to finance and bring in funding for William Garrison's newspaper, the Libertarian, opened his home on Lombard Street as an Underground Railroad depot and opened a school for Black children.

James Forten died in 1842 after living an incredible life. His early years were devoted to providing for his mother, his middle years towards building his fortune and supporting his family and his later years to uplifting his fellow man. He was not only a great inventor, but an even greater man.

Sarah E. Goode was the owner of a furniture store in Chicago, Illinois. Her claim to fame is that she was the first Black Woman to receive a patent.

In an effort to help people maximize their limited space, Goode invented a Folding Cabinet Bed. The Cabinet Bed when folded up resembled a desk which included compartments for stationary and writing instruments. Goode received her patent on July 14, 1885.

Meredith Charles "Flash" Gourdine was born on September 26, 1929 in Newark, New Jersey. His father worked as a painter and janitor and instilled within his son the importance of a strong work ethic. Meredith attended Brooklyn Technical High School and after classes he helped his father on various jobs, often working eight hour days. However, his father believed that education was more important than just developing into a hard worker and he told him "If you don't want to be a laborer all your life, stay in school." Meredith minded his father's advice, excelling in academics. He was also an excellent athlete, competing in track and field and swimming during his senior year. He did well enough in swimming to be offered a scholarship to the University of Michigan, but he turned it down to enter Cornell University. He paid his way through Cornell for his first two years before receiving a track and field scholarship after his sophomore year. He competed in sprints, hurdles and the long jump. Standing 6' and weighing 175 lbs., he starred for his school, winning four titles at the Intercollegiate Association of Amateur Athletes of America championship and led Cornell to a second place finish at the 1952 NCAA Track and Field Championship (The University of Southern California won the meet but boasted 36 athletes while Cornell had only five c). Gourdine was so heralded that he was chosen to represent the United States at the 1952 Summer Olympic Games in Helsinki, Finland. He received a silver medal in the long jump competition, losing to fellow American Jerome Biffle by one and a half inches. "I would have rather lost by a foot," he would later say. "I still have nightmares about it."

After graduating from Cornell with a Bachelor's Degree in Engineering Physics in 1953, he entered the United States Navy as an officer. He soon returned to academia, entering the California Institute of Technology, the recipient of a Guggenheim Fellowship. He received a Ph.D. in Engineering Science in 1960. During his time at Cal. Tech., he served on the Technical Staff of the Ramo-Woolridge Corporation and then as a Senior Research Scientist at the Cal. Tech. Jet Propulsion Laboratory. After graduation, he became a Lab Director for the Plasmodyne Corporation until 1962 when he joined the Curtiss-Wright Corporation, serving as Chief Scientist.

In 1964, Gourdine borrowed $200,000.00 from family and friends and opened Gourdine Laboratories, a research laboratory located in Livingston, New Jersey and at its height he employed 150 people. In 1973, he founded and served as CEO for Energy Innovation, Inc. in Houston, Texas which produced direct-energy conversion devices (converting low-grade coal into inexpensive, transportable and high-voltage electrical energy). His company's performed research and development, specifically in the fields of electrogasdynamics. Electrogasdynamics refers to the generation of energy from the motion of ionized (electrically charged) gas molecules under high pressure. His biggest creation was the Incineraid system, which was used to disperse smoke from burning buildings and could be used to disperse fog on airport runways. The Incineraid system worked by negatively charging smoke or fog, causing the airborne particles within to be electro magnetically charged and then to fall to the ground. The result was clean air and a clear area. He also received patents for the Focus Flow Heat Sink, which was used to cool computer chips as well as for processes for desalinating sea water, for developing acoustic imaging, and for a high-powered industrial paint spray.

Over his career Gourdine held over 30 patents and many of his creations serve as the basis for allergen-filtration devices common to households across the world. He was inducted into the Engineering and Science Hall of Fame in 1994. Towards his latter years, he suffered from diabetes, and lost his sight as well as one leg due to the disease.

Meredith Gourdine died on November 20, 1998, due to complications from multiples strokes. He left behind a legacy of research, design and innovation that will continue to have an impact for many years.

George F. Grant knew what most of us have come to recognize - the average golfer is a hacker, destroying grass courses and terrorizing other golfers, homeowners and passersby with wild, dangerous drives. Although he loved the game, he grew frustrated trying to keep the ball from rolling away from him as he attempted to tee off and did not want to swing at the ball while it was moving , thus sending off a wild shot.

On December 12, 1899, Grant patented a golf tee which raised the golf ball (made of rubber at that time) slightly off of the ground, enabling the player greater control with his wooden club and therefore of the direction and speed of the drive. The tee was made of a small wooden peg with a concave piece of rubber on top to hold the ball and in addition to helping with control over the direction of the shot, it also aided in promoting longer drives.

George Grant's small invention has become a standard piece of equipment for all golfers.

Lloyd Hall was born on June 20, 1894 in Elgin, Illinois. He was an honor student while attending West Side High School in Aurora, Illinois and captained the school debate team while competing in baseball, football and track. Lloyd graduated High School in the top 10 of his class and had to choose between four college scholarship offers. He decided to attend nearby Northwestern University, earning a Bachelor Degree in Pharmaceutical Chemistry in 1916.

While at Northwestern, Hall attended classes with a fellow student named Carroll L. Griffith who would later go on to become the founder of Griffith Laboratories. After graduation, Hall earned a graduate degree from the University of Chicago.

Hall was soon hired by the Western Electric Company through a telephone interview. When he showed up for his first day, however, he was told by a personnel officer that "we don't take niggers." Recovering from this slight, he began working for the Chicago Department of Health as a chemist and was promoted in 1917 to senior chemist. The next year he moved to Ottumwa, Iowa where he held the position of chief chemist at the John Morrell Company. During this time, World War I broke out and Hall received an appointment as Chief Inspector of Powder and Explosives for the United States Ordnance Department.

On September 23, 1919 Lloyd married Myrrhene Newsome, a teacher from Macomb, Illinois. Two years later, the couple moved to Chicago where Lloyd began working for the Boyer Chemical Laboratory where he took the position of chief chemist and focused on the emerging field of food chemistry, and began looking at a way of preserving meats with chemicals. In 1922 he moved on to Chemical Products Corporation where he served as President and Chemical director of their consulting laboratory and often consulted with Griffith Laboratories. In 1925, Hall was offered a position with Griffith Laboratories as chief chemist and director of research. Griffith Laboratories, of course, had been founded by Hall's former classmate Carroll Griffith and after years of moving from company to company, Hall accepted the position and remained there for the next 34 years.

Hall had been working for a number of years exploring different areas of food chemistry and upon joining Griffith Laboratories began looking into methods for preserving foods. Up to that point, foods, and especially meats had been preserved by using sodium chloride (table salt). As well, nitrogen-containing chemicals were also used to preserve meats. It was found that nitrates chemically changed into nitrites and then into nitrous acid which caused the meats to maintain a healthy, red color (the process was referred to as curing meat). Hall found, however, that when sodium chloride, sodium nitrate and sodium nitrite were used in order to preserve and cure the meat, the nitrates and nitrites penetrated the meat much faster than did the sodium chloride. In doing so, the nitrates and nitrites adversely affected the meat by breaking it down before the sodium chloride had a chance to preserve it. In order to correct this, Hall found a while of encasing the nitrates and nitrites within a sodium chloride "shell" by utilizing a process called "flash-drying" the crystals over heated rollers. This allowed the sodium nitrate to be introduced to the meats first and dissolved, and then the nitrates and nitrites were able to penetrate the "preserved" meat and therefore "cure" it.

Hall next addressed a problem which arose when meats were stored in containers. The sodium chloride/nitrate/nitrite combination tended to absorb the moisture from the air inside or the container and caused them to form a caked mass on top of the meat. Hall was able to determine that by adding a glycerin and alkali metal tartrate to the original combination, the glycerin and tartrate would effectively absorb the moisture without "caking" and thus preventing the chloride/nitrate/nitrite combination from absorbing it.

Hall also maintained an interest in sterilizing foods, utensils and tools. Although many people thought that certain spices and flavorings also had the added benefit of preserving foods, Hall found that many of these agents actually exposed the foods to an abundance of germs, molds and bacteria. Hall set out to prevent this while at the same time allowing the spices and flavorings to retain the aroma and color (many of these lost their color and aroma and flavor when exposed to high (sterilizing temperatures.) He eventually found a gas called ethylene oxide, which he introduced to the foods within a vacuumed environment which eliminated the germs and bacteria while maintaining appearances, taste and aroma.

These contributions to food preservation and sterilization revolutionized the way foods were processed, prepared, packed and transported, eliminating spoilage and health hazards and improving efficiency and profitability for food suppliers. In the course of his work, Hall would publish more than 5 scientific papers and receive more than 100 patents. He also served as an advisor to the United States during two World Wars, served on dozens of advisory panels and boards and received hundreds of awards and accolades.

In 1959 Hall retired from Griffith Laboratories and moved to Pasadena, California where he died in 1971. He left behind a legacy as a pioneer in the field of food chemistry and is responsible for improving health conditions in all areas of the food industry.

J. Hawkins developed what are now known as metal oven racks to aid in home cooking. The oven racks were based on gridirons, which were metal racks attached to a wooden handle and were placed on a campfire or placed inside of a fireplace to heat or broil various types of meat. By the early 1800's, gridirons were not used as much as most homes had begun using kitchen stoves upon which to cook.

Hawkins received a patent for the **improved gridiron** on May 26, 1845. The device allowed for different items to be cooked at different level of heat intensity, thus enabling cooks to heat several types of food at once.

Thomas Jennings stands in history as a noteworthy figure for being the first Black person to ever receive a patent, but his life should serve as an example of what was, and what could have been, for Black people in the earliest years of the United States.

Thomas Jennings was born in 1891 and worked in a number of jobs before focusing on what would become his chosen career... as a tailor. Jennings' skills were so admired that people near and far came to him to alter or custom-tailor items of clothing for them. Eventually, Jennings reputation grew such that he was able to open his own store on Church Street which grew into one of the largest clothing stores in New York City.

Jennings, of course, found that many of his customers were dismayed when their clothing became soiled, and because of the material used, were unable to use conventional means to clean them. Conventional methods would often ruin the fabric, leaving the person to either continue wearing the items in their soiled condition or to simply discard them. While this would have provided a boon to his business through increased sales, Jennings also hated to see the items, which he worked so hard to create, thrown away. He thus set out experimenting with different solutions and cleaning agents, testing them on various fabrics until he found the right combination to effectively treat and clean them. He called his method "dry-scouring" and it is the process that we now refer to as dry-cleaning.

In 1820, Jennings applied for a patent for his dry-scouring process. In light of the times, he was fortunate that he was a free man, born in the United States, and thus an American citizen. Under the United States patent laws of 1793 (and later, as revised in 1836) a person must sign an oath or declaration stating that they were a citizen of the United States. While there were, apparently, provisions through which a slave could enjoy patent protection, the ability of a slave to seek out, receive and defend a patent was unlikely. Later, in 1958, the patent office changed the laws, stating that since slaves were not citizens, they could not hold a patent. Furthermore, the court (in the famous case Oscar Stuart vs. Ned case) said that the slave owner, not being the true inventor could not apply for a patent either. In true irony, when many of the southern states seceded from the Union to form the Confederate States of America, CSA President Jefferson Davis signed into law legislation permitting slaves to hold patents. For Thomas Jennings, none of this mattered because as a free man, not only was he able to receive a patent, but he was also to utilize it for his financial gain. In fact, he made a fortune.

What makes Jennings noteworthy is not just that he was an entrepreneur or that he received a patent, or even the fact that he became very wealthy. What is noteworthy is that he took a vast amount of the proceeds of his business and poured it into abolitionist activities throughout the Northeast. In fact, in 1831, he became the assistant secretary for the First Annual Convention of the People of Color in Philadelphia, Pennsylvania. He passed this sense of self-worth to his daughter Elizabeth, who was forced off of a public bus in New York City which she riding to go to church. Because of her father's prominence and wealth, she was able to obtain the best legal representation and hired the law firm of Culver, Parker, and Arthur to sue the bus company and was represented in court by a young attorney named Chester Arthur, who would go on to become the 21st President of the United States. Ms. Jennings would ultimately win her case in front of the Brooklyn Circuit Court in 1855.

Thomas Jennings will go down in history as the first Black person to obtain a patent, but he should rather be seen as an example of a citizen who made the best of his life and sought to use his good fortune to make life better for those around him.

Jack Johnson is one of the most interesting inventors ever, not simply because of his invention but more so because of his celebrated and controversial life. Johnson was born on March 31, 1878 in Galveston, Texas under the name John Arthur Johnson and spent much of his teenage life working on boats and along the city's docks. He began boxing in 1897 and quickly became an accomplished and feared fighter. Standing 6' 1" and weighing 192 lbs., Johnson captured the "Colored Heavyweight Championship of the World" on February 3, 1903 in Los Angeles, California and became the World Heavyweight Champion in 1908. He defeated Tommy Burns for the title and thereby became the first Black man to hold the World Heavyweight Title, a fact that did not endear him to the hearts of white boxing fans. Johnson was extremely confident about his capabilities, and defeated everyone he faced with ease. He also bucked many of the social "rules" of the day and openly dated White women. This eventually got him into trouble in 1912 when he was arrested for violation of the Mann Act, a law often used to prevent Black men from traveling with white women. He was charged with taking his White girlfriend, Lucille Cameron, across state lines across state lines for "immoral purposes." Although he and Lucille married later in the year, he was convicted of the crime by Judge Kenesaw Mountain Landis (who would later become the Commissioner of Major League Baseball) and was sentenced to Federal prison for one year. Before he could be imprisoned, he and Lucille fled to Europe.

Johnson eventually returned to the United States and was sent to Leavenworth Federal Prison in Kansas. While in prison, Johnson found need for a tool which would help tighten of loosening fastening devices. He therefore crafted a tool and eventually patented it on April 18, 1922, calling it a wrench.

Jack Johnson died on June 10, 1946 in an automobile accident in Raleigh, North Carolina and was elected to the Boxing Hall of Fame in 1954. Although many boxing fans are unaware of the life of the first Black Heavyweight Boxing Champion, they probably utilize his invention routinely around their homes.

You don't have to be a rocket scientist to come up with a great idea, but it certainly doesn't hurt. For Lonnie Johnson, a lifetime of achievement and success at various levels on government and private sector projects could not prepare him for the success the he would ultimately achieve - by building a better squirt-gun.

Lonnie Johnson was born on October 6, 1949 in Mobile, Alabama. His father worked as a civilian driver at Brookley Air Force Base, and his mother was a homemaker who worked part time as a nurse's aide. His father taught Robert and his brothers how to repair various household items, prompting the boys to create their own toys. The boys once made a go-kart out of household items and a lawn mower motor. Although his parents were excited about his interest in science and inventing, they weren't prepared for the time he decided to experiment with a rocket fuel he created with sugar and saltpeter which exploded and burned up part of the kitchen. His talents were more refined when he attended Williamson High School and in 1968, as a senior, took part in a national science competition sponsored by the University of Alabama. There he displayed a remote controlled robot named "Linex" which he built from scraps found at a junkyard and parts of his brothers' walkie-talkie and his sisters' reel-to-reel tape recorder. He placed first in the competition and entered Tuskegee University on a mathematics scholarship. At Tuskegee he was elected into the Pi Tao Sigma National Engineering Honor Society and graduated with distinction in 1973 with a Bachelor of Science degree in Mechanical Engineering. He continued on at Tuskegee and received a Master's Degree in Nuclear Engineering in 1975.

After graduation, he took a position at the Savannah River National Laboratory, conducting thermal analysis on plutonium fuel spheres. He later served as a research engineer, developing cooling systems at the Oak Ridge National Laboratory in Oak Ridge, Tennessee. He then joined the Air Force and was assigned to the Air Force Weapons Laboratory in Albuquerque, New Mexico where he served as the Acting Chief of the Space Nuclear Power Safety Section. In 1973, he left the Air Force and took over as Senior Systems Engineer at NASA's Jet Propulsion Laboratory in Pasadena, California. He worked on the Galileo Mission to Jupiter, but returned in 1982 to his military career. He worked at the Strategic Air Command (SAC) facility in Bellevue, Nebraska and then moved to the SAC Test and Evaluation Squadron at Edwards Air Force Base in Edwards, California where he worked on the Stealth Bomber. He also worked as Acting Chief at the Space Nuclear Power Safety Section of the Air Force Weapon Laboratory at Kirkland Air Force Base in New Mexico. A Captain, he was awarded the Air Force Achievement Medal and the Air Force Commendation Medal. In 1987, Johnson returned to his work at the Jet Propulsion Laboratory where he worked on the Mars Observer project, and served as the fault protection engineer on the Saturn Cassini mission project. He later worked as a project engineer for the Kraft mission which studied asteroids.

Earlier, around 1982, he was working on developing a heat pump that would work by circulating water rather than expensive and environmentally unfriendly freon. In his basement at home, he took some tubing with a specially devised nozzle on the other end and connected it to a bathroom sink. When he turned on the faucet, a stream of water shot out of the nozzle across the room with such force that the air currents caused the curtain to move. His first thought was "this would make a great water gun."

Johnson set out to develop a pressurized water gun that was safe enough for children to play with. Water guns at the time were very unsophisticated and cheaply made, able to shoot streams of water about eight feet. Using basic tools, he combined a PVC pipe, a piece of Plexiglas and an empty plastic soda bottle. His invention worked by partially filling a reservoir tank with water and then using a handle to force air into the chamber. When the trigger was pulled, the air pressure would force water to exit through a narrow hole, launching a blast of water more than 25 feet. He called his invention a "pneumatic water gun" and he continue revising it until it could shoot almost 50 feet. When he had developed a working model (which he called the Power Drencher), he and his partner Bruce D'Andrade began trying to market it while trying to secure a patent for it. They first tried to market it to Daisy Manufacturing, the BB Gun manufacturing giant, but no deal could be worked out after two years of negotiations. After securing the patent in 1991 (the toy was now called the Super Soaker), Johnson was introduced to Al Davis, an executive with Larimi Corp. at a New York City Toy Fair. Two weeks later Johnson was in Larimi's headquarters in Philadelphia. The executives watching the demonstration all exclaimed "Wow!" Their only concern was whether anyone would pay $10.00 for a squirt gun. After signing a deal with Johnson's company (Johnson Research and Development Co., Inc.) they would all be in for a big surprise.

Within a year, all involved knew they had a runaway hit. On the popular Tonight Show, host Johnny Carson used a Super Soaker to drench his sidekick Ed McMahon. Within 10 years more than 200 million Super Soakers had been sold. The gun had gone through many modifications and expansions, with new product lines, and became the toy of the decade. Johnson continued inventing and would eventually hold more than 80 patents. For his contributions to science (and in light of his great success with the Super Soaker) Johnson was inducted into the Inventor Hall of Fame in 2000. His company has continued to innovate, creating improved radon detectors, heat pumps and lithium battery products as well as new toy concepts.

Lonnie Johnson didn't have to be a rocket scientist to become a worldwide success.... but it sure gave him something to fall back upon.

On February 5, 1884, W. Johnson patented a device made up of a handle attached to a series of spring-like whisk wires used to help mix ingredients. Prior to his eggbeater, all mixing of ingredients was done by hand. and was quite labor-intensive and time-consuming.

Fred McKinley Jones is certainly one of the most important Black inventors ever based on the sheer number of inventions he formulated as well as their diversity.

Fred Jones was born on May 17, 1893 in Covington, Kentucky. His father was a white railroad worker of Irish descent and his mother was Black. It is believed that his mother died while he was young and Fred was raised by his father. When Fred was eight years old, his father took him to Cincinnati, Ohio to where they visited St. Mary's Catholic Church rectory. Fred's father urged Father Edward A. Ryan to take Fred in, in order to expose him to an environment where he might have a better opportunity for gaining an education. Fred performed chores around the church in return for being fed and housed, cutting the grass, shoveling snow, scrubbing floors and learning to cook. At an early age, Fred demonstrated a great interest in mechanical working, whether taking apart a toy, a watch or a kitchen appliance. Eventually he became interested in automobiles, so much so that upon turning 12 years of age, he ran away from his home at the rectory and began working at the R.C. Crothers Garage.

Initially hired to sweep and clean the garage, Fred spent much of his time observing the mechanics as they worked on cars. His observation, along with a voracious appetite for learning through reading developed within Fred an incredible base of knowledge about automobiles and their inner workings. Within three years, Fred had become the foreman of the garage. The garage was primarily designed to repair automobiles brought in by customers but also served as a studio for building racing cars. After a few years of building these cars, Fred desired to drive them and soon became one of the most well known racers in the Great Lakes region. After brief stints working aboard a steamship and a hotel, Jones moved to Hallock, Minnesota began designing and building racecars which he drove them at local tracks and at county fairs. His favorite car was known as Number 15 and it was so well designed it not only defeated other automobile but once triumphed in a race against an airplane.

On August 1, 1918 Jones enlisted in the 809 Pioneer Infantry of the United States Army and served in France during World War I. While serving, Jones recruited German prisoners of war and rewired his camp for electricity, telephone and telegraph service. After being discharged by the Army, Fred returned to Hallock in 1919. Looking for work, Jones often aided local doctors by driving them around for house calls during the winter season. When navigation through the snow proved difficult, Fred attached skis to the undercarriage of an old airplane body and attached an airplane propeller to a motor and soon whisked around town a high speeds in his new **snow machine**. Over the next few years Fred began tinkering with almost everything he could find, inventing things he could not find and improving upon those he could. When one of the doctors he worked for on occasion complained that he wished he did not have to wait for patient to come into his office for x-ray exams, Jones created a portable x-ray machine that could be taken to the patient. Unfortunately, like many of his early inventions, Jones never thought to apply for a patent for machine and watched helplessly as other men made fortunes off of their versions of the device. Undaunted, Jones set out for other projects, including a radio transmitter, personal radio sets and eventually motion picture devices.

In 1927, Jones was faced with the problem of helping friend convert their silent movie theater into a "talkie" theater. Not only did he convert scrap metal into the parts necessary to deliver a soundtrack to the video, he also devised ways to stabilize and improve the picture quality. When Joe Numero, the head of Ultraphone Sound Systems heard about Fred's devices, he invited Fred to come to Minneapolis for a job interview. After taking a position with the company, Fred began improving on many of the existing devices the company sold. Many of his improvements were so significant, representatives from A.T. & T and RCA sat down to talk with Fred and were amazed at the depth of his knowledge on intricate details, particularly in light of his limited educational background. Around this time, Fred came up with a new idea - an **automatic ticket-dispensing machine** to be used at movie theaters. Fred applied for and received a patent for this device in June of 1939 and the patent rights were eventually sold to RCA.

At some point, Joe Numero was presented with the task of developing a device which would allow large trucks to transport perishable products without them spoiling. Jones set to work and developed a cooling process that could refrigerate the interior of the tractor-trailer. In 1939 Fred and Joe Numero received a patent for the vehicle air-conditioning device which would later be called a Thermo King.

This product revolutionized several industries including shipping and grocery businesses. Grocery chains were now able to import and export products which previously could only have been shipped as canned goods. Thus, the frozen food industry was created and the world saw the emergence of the "supermarket."

In addition to installing the Thermo King refrigeration units in trucks and tractor-trailers, Jones modified the original design so they could be outfitted for trains, boats and ships.

During World War II, the Department of Defense found a great need for portable refrigeration units for distributing food and blood plasma to troops in the field. The Department called upon Thermo King for a solution. Fred modified his device and soon had developed a prototype which would eventually allow airplanes to parachute these units down behind enemy lines to the waiting troops.

For the next 20 years, Fred Jones continued make improvements on existing devices and devised new inventions when necessary to aid the public. Jones died on February 21, 1961 and was posthumously awarded the National Medal of Technology, one of the greatest honors an inventor could receive. Jones was the first Black inventor to ever receive such an honor.

Marjorie Stewart Joyner was born in Monterey, Virginia on October 24, 1896, the granddaughter of a slave and a slave-owner. In 1912, an eager Marjorie moved to Chicago, Illinois to pursue a career in cosmetology. She enrolled in the A.B. Molar Beauty School and in 1916 became the first Black women to graduate from the school. Following graduation, the 20 year old married podiatrist Robert E. Joyner and opened a beauty salon.

She was introduced to Madame C.J. Walker, a well-known Black businesswoman, specializing in beauty products and services. Walker supplied beauty products to a number of the most prominent Black figures of the time, including singer Josephine Baker. With her fame, Ms. Walker was able to open over 200 beauty salon shops across the United States.

After Madame Walker's death in 1919, Marjorie was hired to oversee the Madame C.J. Walker Beauty Colleges as national supervisor.

A dilemma existed for Black women in the 1920's. In order to straighten tightly-curled hair, they could so so only by using a stove-heated curling iron. This was very time-consuming and frustrating as only one iron could be used at a time. In 1926, Joyner set out to make this process faster, easier and more efficient. She imagined that if a number of curling irons could be arranged above a woman's head, they could work at the same time to straighten her hair all at once. According to the Smithsonian Institute, Joyner remembered that "It all came to me in the kitchen when I was making a pot roast one day, looking at these long, thin rods that held the pot roast together and heated it up from the inside. I figured you could use them like hair rollers, then heat them up to cook a permanent curl into the hair." Thus, she sought a solution to not only straighten but also provide a curl in a convenient manner.

Joyner developed her concept by connecting 16 rods to a single electric cord inside of a standard drying hood. A woman would thus wear the hood for the prescribed period of time and her hair would be straightened or curled. After two years Joyner completed her invention and patented it in 1928, calling it the "Permanent Waving Machine." She thus became the first Black woman to receive a patent and her device enjoyed enormous and immediate success. It performed even better than anticipated as the curl that it added would often stay in place for several days, whereas curls from standard curling iron would generally last only one day.

In addition to the success found in Madame Walker's salons, the device was a hit in white salons as well, allowing white patrons to enjoy the beauty of their "permanent curl" or "perm" for days. Although popular, the process could be painful as well, so Marjorie patented a scalp protector that could be used to make the experience more pleasant. This too proved to be a major success. Despite her accomplishments and success, Marjorie received none of the proceeds of her inventions as the patents were created within the scope of her employment with Madame Walker's company, which therefore received all patent rights and royalties. Undeterred, in 1945 Joyner co-founded the United Beauty School Owners and Teachers Association along with Mary Bethune McLeod. She tirelessly helped to raise money for Black colleges and founded the Alpha Chi Pi Omega Sorority and Fraternity in an effort to raise professional standards for beauticians. In 1973, at the age of 77, she was awarded a bachelor's degree in psychology from Bethune-Cookman College in Daytona Beach, Florida.

Marjorie Joyner died on December 7, 1994 at the age of 98. She left behind her a legacy of creativity, ingenuity and selflessness that served to inspire many generations.

Percy Julian was born on April 11, 1899 in Birmingham, Alabama, one of six children. His father, a railroad mail clerk, and his mother, a school teacher stressed education to their children. This emphasis would ultimately prove successful as two sons went on to become physicians and three daughters would receive Masters degrees, but it was son Percy who would become the most successful of the children.

Percy attended elementary school in Birmingham and moved on to Montgomery, Alabama where he attended high school at the State Normal School for Negroes. Upon graduation in 1916, Julian applied to and was accepted into DePauw University in Greencastle, Indiana. At DePauw, he began as a probationary student, having to take higher level high school classes along with his freshman and sophomore course load. He proved himself well, going on to be named a member of the Sigma Xi honorary society as well as a Phi Beta Kappa member. Finally, upon graduation from DePauw in 1920, he was selected as the class valedictorian. Though at the top of his class, he was discouraged from seeking admission into a graduate school, because of potential racial sentiment on the part of future coworkers and employers. Instead, he took the advice of an advisor and took a position as a chemistry teacher at Fisk University, a Black college in Nashville, Tennessee.

After two years at Fisk, Julian was awarded the Austin Fellowship in Chemistry and moved to the distinguished Harvard University in Cambridge, Massachusetts. Finally given an opportunity at graduate level work, Julian excelled. He achieved straight A's, finishing at the top of his class and receiving a Masters Degree in 1923. Even with this success, Julian was unable to obtain a position as a teaching assistant at any major universities because of the perception that White students would refuse to learn under a Black instructor. Thus, he moved on to a teaching position at West Virginia State College for Negroes, though he would not find happiness in this situation. He left West Virginia and served as an associate professor of chemistry at Howard University in Washington, D.C. for two years.

In 1929, Julian qualified for and received a Fellowship from the General Education Board and traveled to Vienna, Austria in pursuit of a Ph.D. degree. While in Vienna, Julian developed a fascination with the soybean and its interesting properties and capabilities. Focusing on organic chemistry, Julian received his Ph.D. in 1931 and returned to the United States and to for a while to Howard University as the head of the school's chemistry department. He soon left Howard and moved back to DePauw where he was appointed a teacher in organic chemistry. At DePauw, he worked with an associate of his from Vienna, Dr. Josef Pikl, on the synthesis of physostigmine, a drug which was used as a treatment for glaucoma. After much work and adversity, Julian was successful and became internationally hailed for his achievement. At this point the Dean of the University sought to appoint Julian to the position as Chair of the chemistry department but was talked out of it by others in the department, again because of concerns over reaction to his race.

In late 1935, Percy Julian decided to leave the world of academics and entered the corporate world by accepting a position with the Glidden Company as chief chemist and the Director of the Soya Product Division. This was a significant development as he was the first Black scientist hired for such a position and would pave the way for other Blacks in the future. The Glidden Company was a leading manufacturer of paint and varnish and was counting on Julian to develop compounds from soy-based products which could be used to make paints and other products. Julian did not disappoint, coming up with products such as aero-foam which worked as a flame retardant and was used by the United States Navy and saved the lives of countless sailors during World War II.

On December 24, 1935, Percy married Anna Johnson and the company settled into their comfortable life in Chicago. Percy continued his success as he next developed a way to inexpensively develop male and female hormones from soy beans. These hormones would help to prevent miscarriages in pregnant women and would be used to fight cancer and other ailments. He next set out to provide a synthetic version of cortisone, a product which greatly relieved the pain of suffered by sufferers of rheumatoid arthritis. The real cortisone was extremely expensive and only rich people could afford it. With Julian's discovery of the soy-based substitute, millions of sufferers around the world found relief at a reasonable price. So significant was his work that in 1950 the City of Chicago named him Chicagoan of the Year. While the honor should have signaled Julian's acceptance by his white counterparts in his field and his community, but when he soon after purchased a home for his family in nearby Oak Park, the home was set afire by an arsonist on Thanksgiving Day 1950. A year later, dynamite was thrown from a passing car and exploded outside the bedroom window of Percy's children. Despite the fact that many residents of the town relied upon his methods to relieve their pains of and provide for their safety, some still could not stand to have him as their neighbor simply because he was Black.

In 1954, Julian left the Glidden Company to establish Julian Laboratories which specialized in producing his synthetic cortisone. When he discovered that wild yams in Mexico were even more effective than Soya beans for some of his products, he opened the Laboratorios Julian de Mexico in Mexico City, Mexico which cultivated the yams and shipped them to Oak Park for refinement. In 1961 he sold the Oak Park plant to Smith, Kline and French, a giant pharmaceutical company and received a sum of 2.3 million dollars, a staggering amount for a Black man at that time.

After years of struggling for respect in his field and his community, Julian finally was recognized as a genius and a pioneer. He received countless award and honors including the prestigious Spingarn Medal from the NAACP and was asked to serve on numerous commissions and advisory boards.

Percy Julian died of liver cancer in 1975 and is known worldwide as a trailblazer, both in the world of chemistry and as an advocate for the plight of Black scientists.

Ernest Just was born on August 14, 1883 in Charleston, South Carolina. His mother worked as a school teacher and his father, a dock worker, died when Ernest was only four years old, forcing him to have to work in the fields after school each day. Because high schools in the South provided such poor education at that time, Ernest's mother decided to send him North to receive better schooling. Through hard work, Ernest was able to earn enough money to attend the Kimball Academy in New Hampshire. The Kimball Academy was an exclusive school and Just proved himself worthy by excelling in his classes. As the editor of the school newspaper and President of the debating team, Ernest completed the four year program in only three, graduating with honors as the valedictorian of his class.

In 1903, Just entered Dartmouth College and decided to become a research biologist specializing in cytology (the study of cells). Learning under the guidance of world famous zoologist William Patten, Just excelled and received degrees in history and biology. Upon graduation in 1907, he had already been elected to the Phi Beta Kappa honors fraternity, was named class valedictorian and was the only member of his class to graduate Magna Cum Laude.

In October 1907, Ernest Just was hired by Howard University in Washington, D.C. and would eventually become the head of the biology department while also heading the physiology department and serving as a member of the Medical School's faculty. With all of these responsibilities, Just was still able to pursue a Ph.D. in Zoology, which he received in 1916 from the University of Chicago. He experimented with the reproductive systems and cells of marine animals in the Marine Biological Laboratory in Woods Hole, Massachusetts. His research and papers on Marine biology were so well received that in 1915, at age 32, Just was awarded the first Spingarn Medal by the National Association for the Advancement of Colored People.

Over the next 20 years, Just would perform studies on marine animals and their eggs as well as on their cell structures. He believed that in learning about healthy cells and cell structures, man could hope to understand and find cures for cellular irregularities and diseases such as sickle cell anemia and cancer. He also researched parthenogenesis (developing marine eggs without fertilization). He quickly became one of the most respected scientists in his field, but much of that recognition came from abroad as racial bigotry in the United States caused much of his work and his achievements to go unrewarded.

In other countries, he was treated as a pioneer, recruited to work with Russian scientists and invited to be a guest worker at the Kaiser Wilhelm Institute for Biology, at the time the world's greatest scientific research laboratory. He was also welcomed with open arms at the Naples Zoological Station in Italy and the Sorbonne in France, where he conducted research and shared his ideas.

Ernest Just died on October 27, 1941 of cancer, leaving behind a wife, Ethel, and three children. He also left behind a world which would eventually recognize him as the most outstanding zoologist of his time.

Lewis Latimer is considered one of the 10 most important Black inventors of all time...

...not only for the sheer number of inventions created and patents secured but also for the magnitude of importance for his most famous discovery. Latimer was born on September 4, 1848 in Chelsea, Massachusetts. His parents were George and Rebecca Latimer, both runaway slaves who migrated to Massachusetts in 1842 from Virginia. George Latimer was captured by his slave owner, who was determined to take him back to Virginia. His situation gained great notoriety, even reaching the Massachusetts Supreme Court. Eventually George was purchased by abolition supporters who set him free.

Lewis served in the United States Navy for the Union during the Civil War, assigned to the U.S.S. Massasoit gunboat and received an honorable discharge on July 3, 1965. After his discharge he sought employment throughout Boston, Massachusetts and eventually gained a position as an office boy with a patent law firm, Crosby and Gould earning $3.00 each week. After observing Latimer's ability to sketch patent drawings, he was eventually promoted to the position of head draftsman earning $20.00 a week. In addition to his newfound success, Latimer found additional happiness when he married Mary Wilson in November of 1873.

In 1874, along with W.C. Brown, Latimer co-invented an improved of a train water closet, a bathroom compartment for railroad trains. Two years later, Latimer would play a part in one of the world's most important inventions.

In 1876, Latimer was sought out as a draftsman by a teacher for deaf children. The teacher had created a device and wanted Lewis to draft the drawing necessary for a patent application. The teacher was Alexander Graham Bell and the device was the telephone. Working late into the night, Latimer worked hard to finish the patent application, which was submitted on February 14, 1876, just hours before another application was submitted by Elisha Gray for a similar device.

In 1880, after moving to Bridgeport, Connecticut, Latimer was hired as the assistant manager and draftsman for U.S. Electric Lighting Company owned by Hiram Maxim. Maxim was the chief rival to Thomas Edison, the man who invented the electric light bulb. The light was composed of a glass bulb which surrounded a carbon wire filament, generally made of bamboo, paper or thread. When the filament was burned inside of the bulb (which contained almost no air), it became so hot that it actually glowed. Thus by passing electricity into the bulb, Edison had been able to cause the glowing bright light to emanate within a room. Before this time most lighting was delivered either through candles or through gas lamps or kerosene lanterns. Maxim greatly desired to improve on Edison's light bulb and focused on the main weakness of Edison's bulb - their short life span (generally only a few days.) Latimer set out to make a longer lasting bulb.

Latimer devised a way of encasing the filament within an cardboard envelope which prevented the carbon from breaking and thereby provided a much longer life to the bulb and hence made the bulbs less expensive and more efficient. This enabled electric lighting to be installed within homes and throughout streets

Latimer applied for a patent for the "Process of Manufacturing Carbons" and it was granted in January 1882. Because he was working at the time for US Electric Lighting Company, he was forced to assign the patent to the company, and thus lost out on the enormous financial rewards which would result. Around this time, Latimer, along with Joseph V. Nichols, received a patent for an improved incandescent lamp which utilized a more efficient way of connecting the carbon filament to the lead wires at the lamp base. Hiram Maxim named this invention the "Maxim Electric Lamp."

Latimer abilities in electric lighting became well known and soon he was sought after to continue to improve on incandescent lighting as well as arc lighting. Eventually, as more major cities began wiring their streets for electric lighting, Latimer was dispatched to lead the planning team. He helped to install the first electric plants in Philadelphia, New York City and Montreal and oversaw the installation of lighting in railroad stations, government building and major thoroughfares in Canada, New England and London.

In 1890, Latimer, having been hired by Thomas Edison, began working in the legal department of Edison Electric Light Company, serving as the chief draftsman and patent expert. In this capacity he drafted drawings and documents related to Edison patents, inspected plants in search of infringers of Edison's patents, conducted patent searches and testified in court proceeding on Edison's behalf. Later that year wrote the worlds' most thorough book on electric lighting, *Incandescent Electric Lighting:*

A Practical Description of the Edison System." Lewis was named one of the charter members of the Edison pioneer, a distinguished group of people deemed responsible for creating the electrical industry. The Edison Electric Lighting would eventually evolve into what is now known as the General Electric Company.

Latimer continued to display his creative talents over then next several years. In 1894 he created a safety elevator, a vast improvement on existing elevators. He next received a patent for Locking Racks for Hats, Coats, and Umbrellas. The device was used in restaurants, hotels and office buildings, holding items securely and allowing owners of items to keep them from getting misplaced or accidentally taken by others. He next created a improved version of a Book Supporter, used to keep books neatly arranged on shelves.

Latimer next devised a method of making rooms more sanitary and climate controlled. He termed his device an Apparatus for Cooling and Disinfecting. The device worked wonders in hospitals, preventing dust and particles from circulating within patient rooms and public areas.

Throughout the rest of his life, Latimer continued to try to devise ways of improving everyday living for the public, eventually working in efforts to improve the civil rights of Black citizens within the United States. He also painted portraits and wrote poetry and music for friends and family.

Lewis Latimer died on December 11, 1928 and left behind a legacy of achievement and leadership that much of the world owes thanks.

Joseph Lee was born in 1849 and lived most of his life in Boston, Massachusetts. Lee was very prominent in the food services industry, having begun working as a boy at a bakery. He soon began preparing, cooking and serving food, eventually opening two successful restaurants in the Boston area. In the late 1890s he owned and managed the Woodland Park Hotel in Newton, Massachusetts for 17 years. In 1902, as a way of maintaining an involvement in the food services industry, Lee opened a catering business called the Lee Catering Company which served the wealthy population of Boylston Street in the Back Bay. At the same time he also operated the Squantum Inn, a summer resort in South Shores specializing in seafood. The catering business was a great success and during this time he became interest in eliminating a situation that had become annoying to him.

Lee became very frustrated at what he saw as a waste of bread which would have to be thrown out if it was as much as a day old. Considered a master cook, Lee had long believed that crumbs from bread was quite useful in preparing food, as opposed to cracker crumbs which many others favored. He decided that instead of simply throwing stale bread away, he would use it to make bread crumbs. He thus set out to invent of device that could automate tearing, crumbling and grinding the bread into crumbs. He was finally successful and patented the invention on June 4, 1895. He used the bread crumbs for various dishes including croquettes, batter for cakes, fried chops, fried fish and more. He soon sold the rights to his bread crumbling machine and the Royal Worcester Bread Crumb Company of Boston soon had the devices in major restaurants around the world.

Not one to rest on his laurels, Lee looked for another way of improving food preparation and invented an automatic bread making machine. The machine not only mixed the ingredients, but also kneaded the dough. The machine was so fast and efficient it was able to perform the tasks of five or six men and did so more hygienically and at a much cheaper cost. It also produced a higher quality product, with a much better taste and texture. He received a patent for the machine, which is the basis for machines still in use today.

Joseph Lee died in 1905 and is an honored pioneer in the food preparation industry.

E. R. Lewis had a problem with people trespassing on his property, especially poachers. Unfortunately, the only way to prevent people from coming on to his land would be to hide out on the property at all hours, day and night.

Lewis solved this problem by developing a spring gun, which he patented on May 3, 1887. The spring gun was made of a metal tube which sat atop a block of wood with a wire attached to a trigger mechanism. The other end of the wire ran across the ground or was stretched across an area and attached to a post or a tree. Anyone disturbing the wire would cause the gun to discharge, thereby shooting the trespasser.

Many patents are developed in response to the frustration involved in having to perform a repetitive task in order to complete a more important one. For J. L. Love, this repetitive task was having to stop writing notes or letters in able to pull out his knife to whittle his pencil down to a point again.

On November 23, 1897, Love patented the pencil sharpener which called for a user to turn a crank and rotor off thin slices of wood from the pencil until a point was formed.

Four years earlier, Love created and patented his Plasterer's Hawk. This device, a flat square piece of board made of wood or metal, upon which plaster or mortar was placed and then spread by plasterers or masons. This device was patented on July 9, 1895.

Sometimes the greatest inventions are those which simplify necessary tasks. Such is the case with Jan Matzeliger - the man who made it possible for ordinary citizens to purchase shoes.

Jan Matzeliger was born in Dutch Guiana (now known as Surinam) in South America. His father was a Dutch engineer and his mother was born in Dutch Guiana and was of African ancestry. His father had been sent to Surinam by the Dutch government to oversee the work going on in the South American country.

At an early age, Jan showed a remarkable ability to repair complex machinery and often did so when accompanying his father to a factory. When he turned 19, he decided to venture away from home to explore other parts of the world. For two years he worked aboard an East Indian merchant ship and was able to visit several countries. In 1873, Jan decided to stay in the United States for a while, landing in Pennsylvania. Although he spoke very little English, he was befriended by some Black residents who were active in a local church and took pity on him. Because he was good with his hands and mechanically inclined, he was able to get small jobs in order to earn a living.

At some point he began working for a cobbler and became interested in the making of shoes. At that time more than half of the shoes produced in the United States came from the small town of Lynn, Massachusetts. Still unable to speak more than rudimentary English, Matzeliger had a difficult time finding work in Lynn. After considerable time, he was able to begin working as a show apprentice in a shoe factory. He operated a McKay sole-sewing machine which was used to attach different parts of a shoe together. Unfortunately, no machines existed that could attach the upper part of a shoe to the sole. As such, attaching the upper part of a shoe to the sole had to be done by hand. The people who were able to sew the parts of the shoe together were called "hand lasters" and expert ones were able to produce about 50 pairs of shoes in a 10 hour work day. They were held in high esteem and were able to charge a high price for their services, especially after they banded together and formed a union called the Company of Shoemakers. Because the hand lasters were able to charge so much money, a pair of shoes was very expensive to purchase. Hand lasters were confident that they would continue to be able to demand high sums of money for their services saying "... no matter if the sewing machine is a wonderful machine. No man can build a machine that will last shoes and take away the job of the laster, unless he can make a machine that has fingers like a laster - and that is impossible." Jan Matzeliger decided they were wrong.

After working all day Matzeliger took classes at night to learn English. Soon, he was able to read well enough to study books on physics and mechanical science. This enabled him to a number of inventions. Lacking sufficient money, he was unable to patent these inventions and watched helplessly as other people claimed to have created the devises and received the financial rewards they brought. Matzeliger did not despair over these situations because he was already thinking of a more important invention - *the shoe laster.*

Watching hand lasters all day, Matzeliger began understanding how they were able to join the upper parts of a shoe to the sole. At night he sat devising methods for imitating the mannerisms of the hand lasters and sketched out rough drawings of a machine that might work in the same manner.

Soon, Matzeliger began putting together a crude working model of his invention. Lacking the proper materials, he used whatever scraps he could find, including cigar boxes, discarded pieces of wood, scrap wire, nails and paper. After six months, he felt he was on the right track but knew he needed better materials in order to take the next steps.

Although he attempted to keep his invention a secret, people found out, including the expert hand lasters he was trying to "compete" with. These people criticized and ridiculed him and tried to dissuade him pursuing his goal. He considered on, however, and decided to try to raise money in order to improve his working model. He was offered $50.00 to sell the device he had created up to that point but turned it down, knowing that if people were interested in buying, he was on the right track.

As he improved the device, other offers of money came in, some as high as $1,500.00. Matzeliger could not bear to part with the device he had put so much work into creating so he held out until he reached a deal to sell a 66% interest in the devices to two investors, retaining the other third interest for himself. With the new influx of cash, Jan finished his second and third models of the machine. At this point he applied for a patent for the device.

Because no one could believe that anyone could create a machine which could duplicate the work of expert lasters, the patent office dispatched a representative to Lynn, Massachusetts to see the device in action. In March 1883, the United States Patent Office issued a patent to Jan Matzeliger for his "Lasting Machine." Within two years, Matzeliger had perfected the machine to that point that it could produce up to 700 pairs of shoes each day (as compared to 50 per day for a hand laster.)

Sadly, Matzeliger would only enjoy his success for a short time, as he was afflicted with tuberculosis in 1886 and died on August 24, 1889 at the age of 37. As a result of his work, shoe manufacturing capabilities increased as did efficiency. This allowed for lower prices for consumers and more jobs for workers. Matzeliger left behind a legacy of tackling what was thought to be an impossible task - making shoes affordable for the masses.

Although the name Elijah McCoy may be unknown to most people, the enormity of his ingenuity and the quality of his inventions have created a level of distinction which bears his name.

Elijah McCoy was born in Colchester, Ontario, Canada on May 2, 1844. His parents were George and Emillia McCoy, former slaves from Kentucky who escaped through the Underground Railroad. George joined the Canadian Army, fighting in the Rebel War and then raised his family as free Canadian citizens on a 160 acre homestead.

At an early age, Elijah showed a mechanical interest, often taking items apart and putting them back together again. Recognizing his keen abilities, George and Emillia saved enough money to send Elijah to Edinburgh, Scotland, where he could study mechanical engineering. After finishing his studies as a "master mechanic and engineer" he returned to the United States, which had just seen the end of the Civil War - and the emergence of the "Emancipation Proclamation."

Elijah moved to Ypsilanti, Michigan but was unable to find work as an engineer. He was thus forced to take on a position as a fireman\oilman on the Michigan Central Railroad. As a fireman, McCoy was responsible for shoveling coal onto fires which would help to produce steam that powered the locomotive. As an oilman, Elijah was responsible for ensuring that the train was well lubricated. After a few miles, the train would be forced to stop and he would have to walk alongside the train applying oil to the axles and bearings.

In an effort to improve efficiency and eliminate the frequent stopping necessary for lubrication of the train, McCoy set out to create a method of automating the task. In 1872 he developed a "lubricating cup" that could automatically drip oil when and where needed. He received a patent for the device later that year. The "lubricating cup" met with enormous success and orders for it came in from railroad companies all over the country. Other inventors attempted to sell their own versions of the device but most companies wanted the authentic device, requesting "the Real McCoy."

In 1868, Elijah had married Ann Elizabeth Stewart. Sadly, Elizabeth passed away just four years later. In 1873, McCoy married again. This time his bride was Mary Eleanor Delaney and the couple would eventually settle into Detroit, Michigan together for the next 50 years.

McCoy remained interested in continuing to perfect his invention and to create more. He thus sold some percentages of rights to his patent to finance the building of a workshop. He made continued improvements to the "lubricating cup." The patent application described the it as a device which *"provides for the continuous flow of oil on the gears and other moving parts of a machine in order to keep it lubricated properly and continuous and thereby do away with the necessity of shutting down the machine periodically."* The device would be adjusted and modified in order to apply it to different types of machinery. Versions of the cup would soon be used in steam engines, naval vessels, oil-drilling rigs, mining equipment, in factories and on construction sites.

In 1916 McCoy created the graphite lubricator which allowed new superheater trains and devices to be oiled. In 1920, Elijah established the "Elijah McCoy Manufacturing Company." With his new company, he improved and sold the graphite lubricator as well as other inventions which came to him out of necessity. He developed and patented a portable ironing board after his wife expressed a need for an easier way of ironing clothes. When he desired an easier and faster way to water his lawn, he created and patented the lawn sprinkler.

In 1922, Elijah and Mary were involved in an automobile accident and both suffered severe injuries. Mary would die from the injuries and Elijah's health suffered for several years until he died in 1929. McCoy left behind a legacy of successful inventions that would benefit mankind for another century and his name would come to symbolize quality workmanship - the Real McCoy!

D. McCree recognized the safety benefits enjoyed by hotels, apartment buildings and office buildings and decided to extend that safety to homeowners. Basing his model on fire escapes being used by bigger buildings, McCree created a portable version made of wood that could be attached to the windowsill of a home, enabling people within to escape from second and third story levels during a fire.

McCree patented the portable fire escape on November 11, 1890 and it is the basis for similar models used today.

D. McCree recognized the safety benefits enjoyed by hotels, apartment buildings and office buildings and decided to extend that safety to homeowners. Basing his model on fire escapes being used by bigger buildings, McCree created a portable version made of wood that could be attached to the windowsill of a home, enabling people within to escape from second and third story levels during a fire.

McCree patented the portable fire escape on November 11, 1890 and it is the basis for similar models used today.

Benjamin Montgomery was born into slavery in 1819 in Loudon County, Virginia. He was sold to Joseph E. Davis, a Mississippi planter. Davis was the older brother of Jefferson Davis who would later serve as the President of the Confederate States of America. After a period time, Davis could see great talent within Montgomery and assigned to him the responsibility of running his general store on the Davis Bend plantation. Montgomery, who by this time had learned to read and write (he was taught by the Davis children), excelled at running the store and served both white customers and slaves who could trade poultry and other items in return for dry goods. Impressed with his knowledge and ability to run the store, Davis placed Montgomery in charge of overseeing the entirety of his purchasing and shipping operations on the plantation.

In addition to being able to read and write, Montgomery also learned a number of other difficult tasks, including land surveying, techniques for flood control and the drafting of architectural plans. He was also a skilled mechanic and a born inventor. At the time commerce often flowed through the rivers connecting counties and states. With differences in the depths of water in different spots throughout the river, navigation could become difficult. If a steamboat were to run adrift, the merchandise would be delayed for days, if not weeks.

Montgomery decided to address the problem and created a propellor that could cut into the water at different angles, thus allowing the boat to navigate more easily though shallow water. Ben attempted to patent the device but the patent was denied on June 10, 1858, on the basis that Ben, as a slave, was not a citizen of the United States, and thus could not apply for a patent in his name. Later, both Joseph and Jefferson Davis attempted to patent the device in their names but were denied because they were not the "true inventor." Ironically, when Jefferson Davis later assumed the Presidency of the Confederacy, he signed into law the legislation that would allow a slaves to receive patent protection for their inventions. On June 28, 1864, Montgomery, no longer a slave, filed a patent application for his devise, but the patent office again rejected his application.

Upon the end of the Civil War, Joseph Davis sold his plantation as well as other properties to Montgomery, along with his son Isaiah. The sale was made based on a long-term loan in the amount of $300,000.00. Benjamin and Isaiah decided to pursue a dream of using the property to establish a community of freed slaves, but natural disasters decimated their crops, leaving them unable to pay off the loan. The Davis Bend property reverted back to the Davis family and Benjamin died the following year. Undeterred, Isaiah took up his father's dream and later purchased 840 acres of land and along with a number of other former slaves, founded the town of Mound Bayou, Mississippi in 1887. Isaiah was named the town first mayor soon thereafter.

While Benjamin Montgomery's story sounds sad in its telling, it served as a lesson to Whites and Blacks in the Civil War period, demonstrating the power of education and the ability for blacks to contribute to commerce and industry in the American south.

Garrett Morgan is one of those rare people who are able to come up with an extraordinary invention which has a tremendous impact on society - and then follows that up with even more!

Garrett Morgan was born on March 4, 1877 in Paris, Kentucky, the seventh of 11 children born to Sydney and Elizabeth Morgan. Garrett, at the early age of 14, decided that he should travel north to Ohio in order to receive a better education. He moved to Cincinnati and then to Cleveland, working as a handyman in order to make ends meet. In Cleveland, he learned the inner workings of the sewing machine and in 1907 opened his own sewing machine store, selling new machines and repairing old ones. In 1908 Morgan married Mary Anne Hassek with whom he would have three sons.

In 1909, Morgan opened a tailoring shop, selling coats, suits and dresses. While working in this shop he came upon a discovery which brought about his first invention. He noticed that the needle of a sewing machine moved so fast that its friction often scorched the thread of the woolen materials. He thus set out to develop a liquid that would provide a useful polish to the needle, reducing friction. When his wife called him to dinner, he wiped the liquid from his hands onto a a piece of pony-fur cloth. When he returned to his workshop, he saw that the fibers on the cloth were now standing straight up. He theorized that the fluid had actually straightened the fibers. In order to confirm his theory, he decided to apply some of the fluid to the hair of a neighbor's dog, an *Airedale*. The fluid straightened the dog's hair so much, the neighbor, not recognizing his own pet, chased the animal away. Morgan then decided try the fluid on himself, to small portions of his hair at first, and then to his entire head. He was successful and had invented the first human-hair straightener. He marketed the product under the name the G. A. Morgan Hair Refining Cream and sold by his G. A Morgan Refining Company, which became a very successful business.

In 1912, Morgan developed another invention, much different from his hair straightener. Morgan called it a *Safety Hood* and patented it as a *Breathing Device*, but the world came to know it as a *Gas Mask*. The Safety Hood consisted of a hood worn over the head of a person from which emanated a tube which reached near the ground and allowed in clean air. The bottom of the tube was lined with a sponge type material that would help to filter the incoming air. Another tube existed which allowed the user to exhale air out of the device. Morgan intended the device to be used *"to provide a portable attachment which will enable a fireman to enter a house filled with thick suffocating gases and smoke and to breathe freely for some time therein, and thereby enable him to perform his duties of saving life and valuables without danger to himself from suffocation. The device is also efficient and useful for protection to engineers, chemists and working men who are obliged to breathe noxious fumes or dust derived from the materials in which they are obliged to work."*

The National Safety Device Company, with Morgan as its General Manager, was set up to manufacture and sell the device and it was demonstrated at various exhibitions across the country. At the Second International Exposition of Safety and Sanitation, the device won first prize and Morgan was award a gold medal. While demonstrations were good for sales, the true test of the product would come only under real life circumstances.

That opportunity arose on July 24, 1916 when an explosion occurred in a tunnel being dug under Lake Erie by the Cleveland Water Works. The tunnel quickly filled with smoke, dust and poisonous gases and trapped 32 workers underground. They were feared lost because no means of safely entering and rescuing them was known. Fortunately someone at the scene remembered about Morgan's invention and ran to call him at his home where he was relaxing. Garrett and his brother Frank quickly arrived at the scene, donned the Safety Hood and entered the tunnel. After a heart wrenching delay, Garrett appeared from the tunnel carrying a survivor on his back as did his brother seconds later. The crowd erupted in a staggering applause and Garrett and Frank reentered the tunnel, this time joined by two other men. While they were unable to save all of the workers, the were able to rescue many who would otherwise have certainly died. Reaction to Morgan's device and his heroism quickly spread across the city and the country as newspapers picked up on the story. Morgan received a gold medal from a Cleveland citizens group as well as a medal from the International Association of Fire Engineers, which also made him an honorary member.

Soon, orders came in from fire and police departments across the country. Unfortunately, many of these orders were canceled when it was discovered that Morgan was Black. Apparently, many people would rather face danger and possibly death than rely on a lifesaving device created by a Black man. Nonetheless, with the outbreak of World War I and the use of poisonous gases therein, Morgan's Safety Hood, now known as the Gas Mask was utilized by the United States Army and saved the lives of thousands of soldiers.

Although he could have relied on the income his Gas Masks generated, Morgan felt compelled to try to solve safety problems of the day. One day he witnessed a traffic accident when an automobile collided with a horse and carriage. The driver of the automobile was knocked unconscious and the horse had to be destroyed. He set out to develop a means of automatically directing traffic without the need of a policeman or worker present. He patented an automatic traffic signal which he said could be "operated for directing the flow of traffic" and providing a clear and unambiguous "visible indicator."

Satisfied with his efforts, Morgan sold the rights to his device to the General Electric Company for the astounding sum of $40,000.00 and it became the standard across the country. Today's modern traffic lights are based upon Morgan's original design.

At that point, Morgan was honored by many influential people around him, including such tycoons as John D. Rockefeller and J.P. Morgan (after whom he named one of his sons.) Although his successes had brought him status and acclaim, Morgan never forgot that his fellow Blacks still suffered injustices and difficulties. His next endeavor sought to address these as he started a newspaper called the Cleveland Call (later renamed as the Call & Post.) He also served as the treasurer of the Cleveland Association of Colored Men which eventually merged with the National Association for the Advancement of Colored People (NAACP) and ran as a candidate for Cleveland's City Council.

In his later years, Morgan would develop glaucoma and would thereby lose 90% of his vision. He died on July 27, 1963 but because of his contributions, the world is certainly a much safer place.

George Murray was without a doubt, one of the most remarkable citizens of his time. A teacher, farmer, land developer and federal customs inspector, the former slave would go on to become a United States Congressman and a noted inventor.

George Murray was born in Sumter County, South Carolina in September, 1853. He spent the first 13 years of his life as a slave, but after the Emancipation Proclamation, he enrolled at South Carolina State University and later continued his education at the State Normal Institute. In the next 20 years he served as a school teacher, the Chairman of the Sumter County Republican Committee and as a customs inspector for the

Port of Charleston, a position he was appointed to by the President of the United States, Benjamin Harrison.

In 1892 George Murray was elected as United States Congressman, representing the state of South Carolina. In this position he frequently spoke from the floor of the House, describing the plight of Black citizens and imploring his fellow Congressmen to protect those citizens rights. One topic that Murray spoke openly about was the plight of the Black inventor. In that day of age, most whites were completely unaware of the success that many Blacks had enjoyed in inventing useful devices which were benefiting ordinary citizens. Murray recounted these achievements and read them into the Congressional Record. While serving in his second term, Murray secured patents for eight inventions, including cultivating and fertilizing equipment and a cotton chopper.

John P. Parker was born in 1827 in Norfolk, Virginia. His father was white and his mother was a black slave. John was sold to a slave agent in 1835 and then sold to a slave caravan which took him to Mobile, Alabama where he was purchased by a physician. Working as a house servant, Parker learned to read and write, often learning alongside of the physician's sons.

In 1843 John was sent North with the owners sons as they went to attend college. John was soon brought back to Mobile when the physician feared he might escape into the Northern territories. Back in Mobile, Parker worked as an craftsman's apprentice for an iron manufacturer and learned to be a plasterer. After being abused by one of his bosses, John attempted to escape to New Orleans but was captured trying to flee by a riverboat and was returned to his owner.

Parker eventually became a molder and was transferred to a New Orleans foundry where he was able to do extra work to earn money. This would allow him to purchase his freedom in 1845 for $1,800.00. At this point he moved north to. Indiana and began working in foundries. At the same time he secretly became a conductor on the "Underground Railroad", eventually helping to smuggle more than 1,000 slaves to escape into free states such as Indiana and Ohio.

In 1848, Parker moved to Beachwood Factory, Ohio where he opened a general store. Six years later he opened a small foundry near Ripley, Ohio which produced special and general castings. The foundry eventually employed more than 25 workers and manufactured slide valve engines and reapers. In 1863 Parker served as a recruiter for the 27th Regiment, U.S Colored troop during the United States Civil War and furnished castings to the war effort.

In 1884 John P. Parker created a screw for Tobacco presses, receiving a patent later in the year.

Robert Pelham was born in January of 1859 in Petersburg, Virginia. His parents, Robert and Frances Pelham, moved the family to Detroit, Michigan in hopes of finding a more favorable atmosphere for their children to receive an education and opportunities for decent employment. While enrolled in public schools, Pelham was hired by a newspaper called the *Daily Post*, working under Zachariah Chandler, who trained him in the skills of journalism. He remained with the paper for 20 years while at the same time managing a Black weekly newspaper called the *Detroit Plaindealer*.

Pelham would later hold a number of important jobs, including Deputy Oil Inspector for the state of Michigan, Special Agent for the United States Land Office and Inspector for the Detroit Water Department. In 1893 Robert married Gabrielle Lewis and the couple moved to Washington, D.C. in 1900 where he took a job as a clerk for the United States Census Department. Studying at night, Pelham received a law degree from Howard University in 1904 and soon began work on a project to help him with his job at the Census Department.

At the Census Department, a clerk had to manually paste statistical slips onto sheets and organized appropriately. The process was messy and required many employees to carry it out. Pelham devised a method for automating the pasting process and set out to create a device that could accomplish it. Starting with a rolling pin, cigar boxes, wooden screws and other miscellaneous items, Pelham developed a working model which he put into effect. The apparatus would go on to save the Department more than $3,000.00 He continued working for the Census Bureau for 30 years, and during that time patented two items - the tabulation device in 1905 and a tallying machine in 1913.

After retiring from the Census Bureau, he began editing a Black newspaper called the Washington Tribune, and later created the Capital News Services, a news agency devoted to Black issues of the day. In June of 1943 Robert Pelham died leaving behind him a list of accomplishments.

W. B. Purvis realized how much of an inconvenience it was to have to carry around a bottle of ink whenever you needed to sign a contract or fill out legal papers. He therefore decided to do something about it.

On January 7, 1890, Purvis received a patent for the fountain pen. The pen eliminated the need for an ink bottle by storing ink within a reservoir within the pen which is then fed to the pen's tip. Of his accomplishment, Purvis said, "the object of my invention is to provide a simple, durable, and inexpensive construction of a fountain pen adapted to general use and which may be carried in the pocket." The creation of the fountain pen has made office work cleaner and less expensive for businesses all over the world.

In addition to his fountain pen, Purvis, a resident of Philadelphia, Pennsylvania, also successfully patented a number of other inventions. Between 1884 and 1897 he patented bag machines, a bag fastener, a hand stamp, an electric railway device, an electric railway switch and a magnetic car balancing device. He also is believed to have invented , yet not patented several other devices such as the edge cutter found on aluminum foil, cling wrap and wax paper boxes.

Before L. P. Ray patented his invention, anyone cleaning a room or a hall simply swept dirt, dust or trash out of a door onto the ground outside or used a piece of paper in order to collect it. Ray created a device with a metal collection plate attached to a short wooden handle in which trash could be swept without getting one's hands dirty.

The device was patented on August 3, 1897 and is called a dustpan.

Andre Reboucas was born in 1838 in Rio de Janeiro, Brazil. He was trained at the Military School of Rio de Janeiro and became an engineer after studying in Europe. After returning to Brazil, Reboucas was named a lieutenant in the engineering corps in the 1864 Paraguayan War. During the war, as naval vessels became more and more integral, Reboucas designed an immersible device which could be projected underwater, causing an explosion with any ship it hit. The device became known as the torpedo.

After his military career, Reboucas began teaching at the Polytechnical School in Rio de Janeiro and became very wealthy. He used his wealth to aid in the Brazilian abolition movement, trying to end slavery in Brazil. After growing disgusted with conditions in Brazil, Reboucas moved to Funchal, Madeira, off of the coast of Africa where he died in 1898.

A. C. Richardson was one of those rare inventors who not only created numerous devices, but created devices that were completely unrelated to one another.

Until 1891 anyone wanting to make butter would have to do so by hand in a bowl. On February 17, 1891 Richardson patented the **butter churn**. The device consisted of a large wooden cylinder container with a plunger-like handle which moved up and down. In doing so, the movement caused oily parts of cream or milk to become separated from the more watery parts. This allowed for an easy way to make butter and forever changed the food industry.

In 1894, Richardson saw a problem with the way the bodies of dead people were buried. It was common at that time to simply bury bodies in small, shallow graves or to try to lower their caskets with ropes into a deeper hole. Unfortunately, this required several people to work in unison to ensure that the casket was lowered evenly. Failure to do so could cause the casket to slip out of one of the ropes and to be damaged from hitting the ground. On November 13, 1894, Richardson patented the **casket lowering device** which consisted of a series of pulleys and ropes or cloths which ensured uniformity in the lowering process. This invention was very significant at that time and is used in all cemeteries today.

In addition to these devices, Richardson patented a hame fastener in 1882, an insect destroyer in February of 1899 and an improvement in the design of the bottle in December of 1899.

Safety, efficiency and profitability - these are the major reasons for the success of an invention. As well, an even greater qualification is when the invention revolutionizes an industry and an overwhelming effect on society. Norbert Rillieux can certainly be seen to have achieved all of these goals

Norbert Rillieux was born on March 17, 1806 in New Orleans, Louisiana. Norbert was born a free man, although his mother was a slave.

His father was a wealthy White engineer involved in the cotton industry. As a child Norbert was educated in the Catholic school system in New Orleans but was sent to Paris, France for advanced schooling. He studied at the L'Ecole Centrale and at age 24 became an instructor of applied mechanics at the school. Eventually Rillieux returned home to his father's plantation which was now also being used to process and refine sugar.

Sugarcane had become the dominant crop within Louisiana, but the sugar refining process employed at that time was extremely dangerous and very inefficient. Known as the "Jamaica Train", the process called for sugarcane to be boiled in huge open kettles and then strained to allow the juice to be separated from the cane. The juice was then evaporated by boiling it at extreme temperatures, resulting in granules being left over in the form of sugar. The danger stemmed from the fact that workers were forced to transport the boiling juice from one one kettle to another, chancing the possibility of of suffering sever burns. It was also a very costly process considering the large amount of fuel needed to heat the various kettles.

During the 1830s, France witnessed the introduction of the steam-operated single pan vacuum . The vacuum pan was enclosed in an area with air of the air removed (this was necessary because liquids can boil at a lower temperature in the absence of air than with air present, thus costing less.) Rillieux decided to improve greatly on this efficiency by including a second and later a third pan, with each getting heating by its predecessor.

In 1833, Rillieux was approached by a New Orleans sugar manufacturer named Edmund Forstall. Because numerous sugar producers had received complaints about product quality, Forstall persuaded Norbert to become the Chief Engineer of the Louisiana Sugar Refinery. Unfortunately, almost as soon as Norbert took the job, an intense feud developed between Forstall and his father, Vincent Rillieux. Out of loyalty to his father, Norbert left his position with the company. A few years later, Norbert was hired by Theodore Packwood to improve his Myrtle Grove Plantation refinery. In doing so he employed his triple evaporation pan system which he patented in 1843. It was an enormous success and revolutionized the sugar refining industry improving efficiency, quality and safety.

In the 1850s, New Orleans was suffering from an outbreak of Yellow Fever, caused by disease-carrying mosquitos. Rillieux devised an elaborate plan for eliminating the outbreak by draining the swamplands surrounding the city and improving the existing sewer system, thus removing the breeding ground for the insects and therefore the ability for them to pass on the disease. Unfortunately, Edmund Forstall, Norbert's former employer was a member of the state legislature and spoke out against the plan. Forstall was able to turn sentiment against Rillieux and the plan was rejected. Disgusted will the racism prevalent in the south as well as the frustration of local politics Rillieux eventually left New Orleans and moved back to France (ironically, after a number of years in which time the Yellow Fever continued to devastate New Orleans, the state legislature was forced to implement an almost identical plan introduced by white engineers.

After returning to France, Rillieux spent much of his time creating new inventions and defending his patents as well as traveling abroad. Rillieux died on October 8, 1894 and left behind a legacy of having revolutionized the sugar industry and therefore changing the way the world would eat.

Inventors often toil for their entire lifetimes creating devices which have beneficial effects on society for years - yet that inventor might gain recognition only after he or she has passed away. For others, even after they have gone, recognition is slow in coming despite their great contributions. Richard Spikes is such a person.

Little has been written about Richard Spikes in terms of his childhood, education and personal life. What is known is that he was an incredible inventor and the proof of this is in the incredibly diverse number of creations that have had a major impact on the lives of everyday citizens.

railroad semaphore (1906)
automatic car washer (1913)
automobile directional signals (1913)
beer keg tap (1910)
self-locking rack for billiard cues (1910)
continuous contact trolley pole (1919)
combination milk bottle opener and cover (1926)
method and apparatus for obtaining average samples and temperature of tank liquids (1931)
automatic gear shift (1932)
transmission and shifting thereof (1933)
automatic shoe shine chair (1939)
multiple barrel machine gun (1940)
horizontally swinging barber chair (1950)
automatic safety brake (1962)

Spikes inventions were welcome to major companies. His beer keg tap was purchased by Milwaukee Brewing Company and the automobile directional signals which were first introduced in the Pierce Arrow, soon became standard in all automobiles. For his innovative designs of transmission and gear-shifting devices, Spikes received over $100,000.00 - an enormous sum for a Black man in the 1930s.

By the time he was creating the automatic safety brake in 1962, Spikes was losing his vision. In order to complete the device, he first created a drafting machine for blind designers - by the time his braking device was completed, he was deemed legally blind. The device would soon be found in almost every school bus in the nation.

Richard Spikes died in 1962 but left behind a lifetime of achievement that few could parallel.

Many inventions were born from necessity and others for convenience. Others, however, are designed to lessen the drudgery and unpleasentness of daily tasks. Such was the invention of Thomas Stewart.

Cleaning floors had always meant scrubbing them on your hands and knees using a scrub brushes and rags. Thomas Stewart envisioned an easier, less painful way. Using a cloth connected to a stick handle and held in place by a metal clasp, Stewart present the world with invention of the mop.

Lewis Temple was born in 1800 as a slave in Richmond, Virginia. He obtained his freedom and moved to New Bedford, Massachusetts in 1929 where he worked as a blacksmith.

Later that year he married Mary Clark, with whom he would later have three children. He also opened a whalecraft store although he had no experience with whaling or as a seaman. In 1845, Temple was enjoying so much success that he was able to open a larger whalecraft store.

The New England region was the capital of the whaling industry. Whale meat and oil was very valuable and the industry provided jobs to seamen and seafront businesses. A big concern for these people was the inability to develop a surefire method of successfully hunting whales. The existing methods of the day often ended in failure as the whales were disengage themselves from the whalers harpoons by spinning and thrashing about.

In 1848 Temple set out to make an improved harpoon that could withstand the enormous strength of the large mammals and would be difficult to escape from. He developed a harpoon with a pivoting head that stayed embedded within the creature. Calling the invention Temple's Toggle or Temple's Iron, the harpoon was actually very similar to hunting tolls used by whale hunters during prehistoric times. His harpoon became a great success, but he never patented it. As such, many blacksmiths began copying the device and selling it as their own. Nonetheless, he enjoyed enough success that he needed to build an even larger shop.

Unfortunately, in 1854 while the new shop was under construction, Temple hell into a whole near the shop and was unable to work. The hole was the result of construction by the city and Temple successfully sued and was awarded $2,000.00 by the court. He never received any of the payment, for he died a few short weeks later as a result of his injuries. All of the profits he had made on his harpoon and his business went to paying for his debts and his family was unable to collect on the money awarded by the court - a strange and ironic tragedy that a made who did so much for the town during his life, would be ignored in death.

Though the City of New Bedford did not recognize their obligation to debt to him at his death, the industry owed him much more because of his invention. Experts after his death agreed with Clifford Ashley, who announced that his Temple's harpoon was "the single most important invention in the whole history of whaling."

As a child, Valerie Thomas became fascinated with the mysteries of technology, tinkering with electronics with her father and reading books on electronics written for adolescent boys. The likelihood of her enjoying a career in science seemed bleak, as her all-girls high school did not push her to take advanced science or math classes or encourage her in that direction. Nonetheless, her curiosity was piqued and upon her graduation from high school, she set out on the path to become a scientist.

Thomas enrolled at Morgan State University and performed exceedingly well as a student, graduating with a degree in physics (one of only two women in her class to do so). She accepted a position with the National Aeronautics and Space Administration (NASA), serving as a data analyst. After establishing herself within the agency, she was asked to manage the

"Landsat" project, an image processing system that would allow a satellite to transmit images from space.

In 1976 Thomas attended a scientific seminar where she viewed an exhibit demonstrating an illusion. The exhibit used concave mirrors to fool the viewer into believing that a light bulb was glowing even after it had been unscrewed from its socket. Thomas was fascinated by what she saw, and imagined the commercial opportunities for creating illusions in this manner.

In 1977 she began experimenting with flat mirrors and concave mirrors. Flat mirrors, of course, provide a reflection of an object which appear to lie behind the glass surface. A concave mirror, on the other hand, presents a reflection that appears to exist in front of the glass, thereby providing the illusion that they exist in a three-dimensional manner. Thomas believed that images, presented in this way could provide a more accurate, if not more interesting, manner of representing video data. She not only viewed the process as a potential breakthrough for commercial television, but also as scientific tool for NASA and its image delivery system.

Thomas applied for a patent for her process on December 28, 1978 and the patent was issued on October 21, 1980. The invention was similar to the technique of holographic production of image recording which uses coherent radiation and employs front wave reconstruction techniques which render the process unfeasible due to the enormous expense and complicated setup. Parabolic mirrors, however, can render these optical illusions with the use use of a concave mirror near the subject image and a second concave mirror at a remote site. In the description of her patent, the process is explained. "Optical illusions may be produced by parabolic mirrors wherein such images produced thereby are possessed with three dimensional attributes. The optical effect may be explained by the fact that the human eyes see an object from two view points separated laterally by about six centimeters. The two views show slightly different spatial relationships between near and near distant objects and the visual process fuses these stereoscopic views to a single three dimensional impression. The same parallax view of an object may be experienced upon reflection of an object seen from a concave mirror." (http://www.freepatentsonline.com/4229761.html). The Illusion Transmitter would thus enable the users to render three-dimensional illusions in real-time.

Valerie Thomas continued working for NASA until 1995 when she retired. In addition to her work with the Illusion Transmitter she designed programs to research Halley's comet and ozone holes. She received numerous awards for her service, including the GSFC Award of Merit and the NASA Equal Opportunity Medal. In her career, she showed that the magic of fascination can often lead to concrete scientific applications for real-world problem-solving.

In 1935, Benjamin Thornton created a device that could be attached to a telephone and could be set to record a voice message from a caller. By utilizing a clock attachment, the machine could also forward the messages as well as keep track of the time they were made.

This device was the predecessor of today's answering machine.

Madame C. J. Walker was born on December 23, 1867 in Delta, Louisiana, the daughter of Owen and Minerva Breedlove. Her parents were former slaves working as sharecroppers and both died when Sarah was a child. As a result, Sarah was forced to move from one household to another. At age seven, she moved in with her sister Louvina and her husband. After suffering abuse from Louvina's husband, Sarah ran away and married Moses McWilliams when she was 14 years old. In 1885, she gave birth to their daughter Lelia. Two years later, Moses was murdered by a White lynch mob.

After this tragedy, Sarah moved with her daughter to St. Louis, Missouri where she worked as a cook and housecleaner. Unfortunately, all of the stress and hardship had begun to take its toll on her and she found her hair falling out. She tried several products which claimed would help her condition but to no avail. At this point Sarah had a dream in which a "big Black man appeared to me and told me what to mix up for my hair. Some of the remedy was grown in Africa, but I sent for it, put it on my scalp, and in a few weeks my hair was coming in faster than it had ever fallen out." After she shared her formula with some friends and found it successful for them as well, she realized that there were almost no hair products available for Blacks. She therefore decided to go into business, selling hair products to Black women.

In 1905 Sarah's brother died and she moved to Denver, Colorado to live with her sister-in-law. When she arrived in Denver she had only $2.00 in her pocket yet she worked during the day as a cook in order to finance her part time business. At this point she met Charles Joseph "C.J." Walker, a newspaperman with an innate ability for marketing. She married Walker on January 4, 1906 and the couple set up the "Madam CJ Walker Manufacturing Company" and began placing advertisements in Black newspapers throughout the United States. Although they proved a successful team, they disagreed as to how much the company should grow. After years of struggling and suffering, Sarah wanted her company to grow immensely and divorced him in order to devote herself to the business (he stayed on as a sales agent for the company.). She continued on with many of the ideas he had passed on to her, including going door-to-door to sell the products. Her hard work paid off and in 1906 she brought her daughter Lelia, a recent college graduate, in to manage the company.

While Lelia ran much of the company, Sarah traveled across the country and throughout Latin America and the Caribbean marketing the products and developing new ones. She also sought to bring more women into the company, desiring to empower them and give them a way of rising above the constraints set by a male dominated society.

In 1908, Sarah started Lelia College in Pittsburgh, Pennsylvania, which trained women to sell her products door-to-door and by 1910 had more than 1,000 sales agents. In that year, she moved the company's headquarters to Indianapolis, Indiana and soon the company grew beyond anyone's expectations. By 1914, the woman who only nine years earlier had only $2.00 to her name was now worth more than one million dollars. Her products ranged from hair conditioners and facial creams to hot combs specially made for the hair of Black consumers.

After her early suffering and poverty plagued existence, Sarah McWilliams had looked for a way out and as Madame C.J. Walker was able to purchase a 34 room mansion built off of the Hudson River in New York. When she died on May 25, 1919, she was mourned throughout the Black community as a pioneer and a Black industrialist. For many women, White and Black, however, she had served as an inspiration and a role model.

James Edward West was born on February 10, 1931 in Prince Edward County, Virginia. He was an inquisitive young boy, fascinated with electronics and always ready to take things apart to discover how they worked. His curiosity almost got the better of him when he was eight years old and decided repair a broken radio. Confident that he had fixed the radio, he plugged it into a ceiling outlet, standing on the brass footboard of his bed. Unfortunately, a bolt of 120 volts of electricity shot through his body, temporarily paralyzing him where he stood. Fortunately his brother was standing nearby and knocked him onto the floor, terminating the shock he was receiving. Undeterred, rather than being afraid he became even further intrigued by electronics and electricity.

Although his father had encouraged him to pursue an education, he pushed him to go to medical school, noting that very few Blacks were ever hired by universities for science oriented careers. His father was afraid that James was "taking the long road toward working at the post office." After graduating from high school, however, West enrolled at Temple University in 1953 and received a Bachelor of Science degree in Physics in 1957. While in school, he had worked during the summers as an intern for the Acoustics Research Department at Bell Laboratories in Murray Hills, New Jersey. Upon graduation he was hired by Bell Labs in a full-time position as an acoustical scientist specializing in electro-acoustics, physical and architectural acoustics.

In 1960, West was teamed up with Gerhard M. Sessler, a German-born physicist, and the two were tasked to develop an inexpensive, highly sensitive and compact microphone. At the time, condenser microphones were used in most telephones, but were expensive to manufacture and necessitated the use of a large battery source. Microphones convert sound waves into electrical voltages, thus allowing the sound to be transmitted through a cord to a receiver.

Because of the associated expense of condenser microphones, they were impractical for everyday home usage. West and Sessler decided to use an electret (an electrical insulator material) using an inexpensive film made of teflon and stretched it taut so that it hung over the top of a metal surface. After being exposed to an electrical field, the electret was able to hold its charge. As West described, "as you talk into the microphone, pressure fluctuations in the air distort the film. Charges in the metal surface experience fluctuating forces as the polarized electret moves above it. As a result of these forces, a very small current flows from the metal surface through a wire that touches it." Their electret microphone solved every problem they were seeking to address. It was inexpensive, could hold a charge without having to be connected to a power source, was compact and durable and could be applied to common uses in the office or in the home. The final model was finished in 1962 and on January 14, 1964, the pair received patent number 3,118,022 for their "electro-acoustic transducer." By 1968, the microphone was in wide scale production and was quickly adopted as the industry standard. Approximately 90% of microphones in use today are based on this invention and almost all telephones utilize it, as well as tape recorders, camcorders, baby monitors and hearing aids.

While the foil-electret microphone was his most noted invention, West obtained more than 100 U.S. and foreign patents over his lifetime and contributed to hundreds of technical papers and books on acoustics and physics. Perhaps his most significant contributions are his efforts to increase minority and female participation in the field of science. He has headed numerous programs with Bell Labs (founding member of the Association of Black Labs Employees) and upon retiring from the company in 2001 (as a Bell Labs Fellow), he became a research professor at Whiting School of Engineering at Johns Hopkins University (where he serves on the Divisional Diversity Council.

James West received many honors during his career, including being inducted into the Inventor's Hall of Fame in 1999, Inventor of the Year (by the state of New Jersey) in 1995, elected as the President of the Acoustical Society of America in 1998 and elected to the National Academy of Engineering the same year. In 2000, he was awarded an honorary Doctorate of Science by the New Jersey Institute of Technology. He undoubtedly is proud that he was able to exceed his father's expectations.

Daniel Hale Williams was born on January 18, 1856 in Hollidaysburg, Pennsylvania. He was the fifth of seven children born to Daniel and Sarah Williams. Daniel's father was a barber and moved the family to Annapolis, Maryland but died shortly thereafter of tuberculosis. Daniel's mother realized she could not manage the entire family and sent some of the children to live with relatives. Daniel was apprenticed to a shoemaker in Baltimore but ran away to join his mother who had moved to Rockford, Illinois. He later moved to Edgerton, Wisconsin where he joined his sister and opened his own barber shop. After moving to nearby Janesville, Daniel became fascinated with a local physician and decided to follow his path. He began working as an apprentice to the physician (Dr. Henry Palmer) for two years and in 1880 entered what is now known as Northwestern University Medical School. After graduation from Northwestern in 1883, he opened his own medical office in Chicago, Illinois.

Because of primitive social and medical circumstances existing in that era, much of Williams early medical practice called for him to treat patients in their homes, including conducting occasional surgeries on kitchen tables. In doing so, Williams utilized many of the emerging antiseptic, sterilization procedures of the day and thereby gained a reputation for professionalism. He was soon appointed as a surgeon on the staff of the South Side Dispensary and then a clinical instructor in anatomy at Northwestern. In 1889 he was appointed to the Illinois State Board of Health and one year later set out to create an interracial hospital.

On January 23, 1891 Daniel Hale Williams established the Provident Hospital and Training School Association, a three story building which held 12 beds and served members of the community as a whole. The school also served to train Black nurses and utilized doctors of all races. Within its first year, 189 patients were treated at Provident Hospital and of those 141 saw a complete recovery, 23 had recovered significantly, three had seen change in their condition and 22 had died. For a brand new hospital, at that time, to see an 87% success rate was phenomenal considering the financial and health conditions of the patient, and primitive conditions of most hospitals. Much can be attributed to Williams insistence on the highest standards concerning procedures and sanitary conditions.

Two and a half years later, on July 9, 1893, a young Black man named James Cornish was injured in a bar fight, stabbed in the chest with a knife. By the time he was transported to Provident Hospital he was seeping closer and closer to death, having lost a great deal of blood and having gone into shock. Williams was faced with the choice of opening the man's chest and possibly operating internally when that was almost unheard of in that day in age. Internal operations were unheard of because any entrance into the chest or abdomen of a patient would almost surely bring with it resulting infection and therefore death. Williams made the decision to operate and opened the man's chest. He saw the damage to the man's pericardium (sac surrounding the heart) and sutured it, then applied antiseptic procedures before closing his chest. Fifty one days later, James Cornish walked out of Provident Hospital completely recovered and would go on to live for another fifty years. Unfortunately, Williams was so busy with other matters, he did not bother to document the event and others made claims to have first achieved the feat of performing open heart surgery. Fortunately, local newspapers of the day did spread the news and Williams received the acclaim he deserved. It should be noted however that while he is known as the first person to perform an open heart surgery, it is actually more noteworthy that he was the first surgeon to open the chest cavity successfully without the patient dying of infection. His procedures would therefore be used as standards for future internal surgeries.

In February 1894, Daniel Hale Williams was appointed as Chief Surgeon at the Freedmen's Hospital in Washington, D.C. and reorganized the hospital, creating seven medical and surgical departments, setting up pathological and bacteriological units, establishing a biracial staff of highly qualified doctors and nurses and established an internship program. Recognition of his efforts and their success came when doctors from all over the country traveled to Washington to view the hospital and to sit in on surgery performed there. Almost immediately there was an astounding increase in efficiency as well as a decrease in patient deaths.

During this time, Williams married Alice Johnson and the couple soon moved to Chicago after Daniel resigned from the Freedmen's hospital. He resumed his position as Chief Surgeon at Provident Hospital (which could now accommodate 65 patients) as well as for nearby Mercy Hospital and St. Luke's Hospital, an exclusive hospital for wealthy White patients. He was also asked to travel across the country to attend to important patients or to oversee certain procedures.

When the American Medical Association refused to accept Black members, Williams helped to set up and served as Vice-President of the National Medical Association. In 1912, Williams was appointed associate attending surgeon at St. Luke's and worked there until his retirement from the practice of medicine.

Upon his retirement, Daniel Hale Williams had bestowed upon him numerous honors and awards. He received honorary degrees from Howard and Wilberforce Universities, was named a charter member of the American College of Surgeons and was a member of the Chicago Surgical Society.

Williams died on August 4, 1931, having set standards and examples for surgeons, both Black and White, for years to come.

The magnitude of an inventors work can often be defined by the esteem in which he is held by fellow inventors. If this is the case, then Granville Woods was certainly a respected inventor as he was often referred to as the "Black Thomas Edison."

Granville Woods was born on April 23, 1856 in Columbus, Ohio. He spent his early years attending school until the age of 10 at which point he began working in a machine shop repairing railroad equipment and machinery. Intrigued by the electricity that powered the machinery, Woods studied other machine workers as they attended to different pieces of equipment and paid other workers to sit down and explain electrical concepts to him. Over the next few years, Woods moved around the country working on railroads and in steel rolling mills. This experience helped to prepare him for a formal education studying engineering (surprisingly, it is unknown exactly where he attended school but it is believed it was an eastern college).

After two years of studying, Woods obtained a job as an engineer on a British steamship called the *Ironsides*. Two years later he obtained employment with D & S Railroads, driving a steam locomotive. Unfortunately, despite his high aptitude and valuable education and expertise, Woods was denied opportunities and promotions because of the color of his skin. Out of frustration and a desire to promote his abilities, Woods, along with his brother Lyates, formed the Woods Railway Telegraph Company in 1884.

The company manufactured and sold telephone, telegraph and electrical equipment. One of the early inventions from the company was an improved steam boiler furnace and this was followed up by an improved telephone transmitter which had superior clarity of sound and could provide for longer range of distance for transmission.

In 1885, Woods patented an apparatus which was a combination of a telephone and a telegraph. The device, which he called "telegraphony," would allow a telegraph station to send voice and telegraph messages over a single wire. The device was so successful that he later sold it to the American Bell Telephone Company. In 1887, Woods developed his most important invention to date - a device he called Synchronous Multiplex Railway Telegraph. A variation of the "**induction telegraph**," it allowed for messages to be sent from moving trains and railway stations. By allowing dispatchers to know the location of each train, it provided for greater safety and a decrease in railway accidents.

Granville Woods often had difficulties in enjoying his success as other inventors made claims to his devices. Thomas Edison made one of these claims, stating that he had first created a similar telegraph and that he was entitled to the patent for the device. Woods was twice successful in defending himself, proving that there were no other devices upon which he could have depended or relied upon to make his device. After the second defeat, Edison decided that it would be better to work with Granville

Woods than against him and thus offered him a position with the Edison Company.

In 1892, Woods used his knowledge of electrical systems in creating a method of supplying electricity to a train without any exposed wires or secondary batteries. Approximately every 12 feet, electricity would be passed to the train as it passed over an iron block. He first demonstrated the device as an amusement apparatus at the Coney Island amusement park and while it amused patrons, it would be a novel approach towards making safer travel for trains.

Many of Woods inventions attempted to increase efficiency and safety railroad cars, Woods developed the concept of a third rail which would allow a train to receive more electricity while also encountering less friction. This concept is still used on subway train platforms in major cities in the United States.

Over the course of his life time Granville Woods would obtain more than 50 patents for inventions including an automatic brake and an egg incubator and for improvements to other inventions such as safety circuits, telegraphs, telephones, and phonographs. When he died on January 30, 1910 in New York City he had become an admired and well respected inventor, having sold a number of his devices to such giants as Westinghouse, General Electric and American Engineering - more importantly the world knew him as the *Black Thomas Edison*.

Cont'd from page 51
Answers: 1-A, 2-D, 3-C, 4-B, 5-C, 6-B, 7-D, 8-A
,9-A, 10-B

What is Black History Month?
Culture - Black History Month
Monday, 11 September 2006 05:03
It is the month in which we bear witness to the progress, richness and diversity of Black achievement. It should be seen as a time for black people to reflect on how far we have come and how far we still have to go. It is a time for Black people all over to reflect on both the history and teachings of Black people whose contributions are still too little known.

FOUNDING OF BLACK HISTORY MONTH

In 1915, historian Carter G. Woodson proposed a "Negro History Week" to honor the history and contributions of African Americans.

Nine years later, his dream became reality. Woodson chose the second week in February to pay tribute to the birthdays of two Americans that dramatically affected the lives of Blacks: Abraham Lincoln (February 12) and Frederick Douglas (February 14). The week-long observance officially became Black History Month in 1976.

BLACK PEOPLE IN BRITAIN BEFORE THE WINDRUSH.

Jeffrey Green argues that to ignore the diverse black presence in Britain prior to the 1940s is to perpetuate a distorted a view of British history..

How do we explain the widespread ignorance of the presence of people of African and Caribbean origin in British history?

Black men and women appear, for example, in Pepy's diaries; in eighteenth-century portraits; sailing with Captain Cook on the Endeavour; not to mention the stories of Thackeray, Trollope, Dornford Yates, W.S. Gilbert, Laurie Lee and Evelyn Waugh. Yet there is a general misapprehension that people of African descent were absent from Britain until recently. This misconception has been nurtured by a belief that apparent exceptions can be ignored.

There is a further mistaken belief that those black people who do appear were temporary residents - and often worked in unskilled occupations - and this added to the notion that they made little contribution to British society.

In 1998, celebrations were held for the half-century anniversary of the arrival of the immigrant ship Empire Wind rush from Jamaica, but these often merely re-confirmed the prejudice that the black presence in Britain was recent, alien and working-class.

EVIDENCE

However, a study of the historic evidence reveals that people of African birth and descent lived in Britain four centuries before the Windrush reached Tilbury.

They and their descendants usually conformed to the prevailing social rules in language, education, style and ambitions, and, accordingly, are to be found at every level of British society. These men, women and children were widespread geographically, even though it is not possible to gauge their overall numbers. But investigations restricted to cities such as London, Cardiff, Liverpool, Glasgow, Tyneside only add to the mistaken stereotype of a foreign-born black working class living in urban ghetto communities.

The assumption that black people were largely absent from Britain until the arrival of Windrush cannot be successfully challenged until it is realized that black people had as broad a range of experiences in Britain as others. For more information and pictures about the historical presence of black people in Britain call the McKenzie Heritage Picture Archives at 020 8469 2000 or visit their website at http://www.mckenziehpa.com.

Historically Black Colleges and Universities

In the late 19th century, colleges for black students were started in box cars (Atlanta University) and church basements (Spelman College). Mary McLeod Bethune, one of the nation's foremost black educators, opened a college in 1904 with $1.50 and 5 students. Today, there are 106 historically black colleges and universities in the United States, who can count among their graduates such luminaries as W. E. B. Du Bois (Fisk University), Thurgood Marshall (Lincoln University and Howard University), Toni Morrison (Howard University), and Martin Luther King, Jr. (Morehouse College).

* Alabama A&M University (Ala.), www.aamu.edu

* Alabama State University (Ala.), www.alasu.edu

* Albany State University (Ga.), www.asurams.edu

* Alcorn State University (Miss.), www.alcorn.edu

* Allen University (S.C.), www.allenuniversity.edu

* Arkansas Baptist College (Ark.), www.arbaptcol.edu

* Barber-Scotia College (N.C.), www.b-sc.edu/

* Benedict College (S.C.), www.benedict.edu

* Bennett College (N.C.), www.bennett.edu

* Bethune-Cookman College (Fla.), www.bethune.cookman.edu

* Bishop State Community College (Ala.) www.bscc.cc.al.us

* Bluefield State College (W.Va.), www.bluefield.wvnet.edu

* Bowie State University (Md.), www.bowiestate.edu

* Central State University (Ohio), www.centralstate.edu

* Charles Drew University of Medicine (Calif.), www.cdrewu.edu

* Cheyney University (Pa.), www.cheyney.edu

* Chicago State University (Ill.) www.csu.edu

* Claflin College (S.C.), www.claflin.edu

* Clark Atlanta University (Ga.), www.cau.edu

* Clinton Junior College (S.C.) www.clintonjrcollege.org

* Coahoma Community College (Miss.) www.ccc.cc.ms.us

* Concordia College (Ala.) www.concordiaselma.edu

* Coppin State College (Md.), www.coppin.edu

* Delaware State University (Del.), www.desu.edu

* Denmark Technical College (S.C.) www.den.tec.sc.us

* Dillard University (La.), www.dillard.edu

* Edward Waters College (Fla.), www.ewc.edu

* Elizabeth City State University (N.C.), www.ecsu.edu

* Fayetteville State University (N.C.), www.uncfsu.edu

* Fisk University (Tenn.), www.fisk.edu

* Florida A&M University (Fla.), www.famu.edu

* Florida Memorial College (Fla.), www.fmc.edu

* Fort Valley State University (Ga.), www.fvsu.edu

* Grambling State University (La.), www.gram.edu

* Hampton University (Va.), www.hamptonu.edu

* Harris-Stowe State College (Mo.), www.hssc.edu

* Hinds Community College (Miss.) lrc.hindscc.edu

* Howard University (D.C.), www.howard.edu

* Huston-Tillotson College (Tex.), www.htc.edu

* Interdenominational Theological Center (Ga.), www.itc.edu

* J. F. Drake State Technical College (Ala.) www.dstc.cc.al.us

* Jackson State University (Miss.), www.jsums.edu

* Jarvis Christian College (Tex.), www.jarvis.edu

* Johnson C. Smith University (N.C.), www.jcsu.edu

* Kentucky State University (Ky.), www.kysu.edu

* Knoxville College (Tenn.), www.knoxvillecollege.edu

* Lane College (Tenn.), www.lanecollege.edu

* Langston University (Okla.) www.lunet.edu

* Lawson State Community College (Ala.) www.ls.cc.al.us

* LeMoyne-Owen College (Tenn.), http://www.loc.edu/index.htm

* Lewis College of Business (Mich.), www.lewiscollege.edu

* Lincoln University (Mo.), www.lincolnu.edu

* Lincoln University (Pa.), www.lincoln.edu

* Livingstone College (N.C.), www.livingstone.edu

* Mary Holmes College (Miss.) www.maryholmes.edu

* Meharry Medical College (Tenn.), www.mmc.edu

* Miles College (Ala.), www.miles.edu

* Mississippi Valley State University (Miss.), www.mvsu.edu

* Morehouse College (Ga.), www.morehouse.edu

* Morehouse School of Medicine (Ga.), www.msm.edu

* Morgan State University (Md.), www.morgan.edu

* Morris Brown College (Ga.)

* Morris College (S.C.), www.morris.edu

* Norfolk State University (Va.), www.nsu.edu

* North Carolina A&T State University (N.C.), www.ncat.edu

* North Carolina Central University (N.C.), www.nccu.edu

* Oakwood College (Ala.), www.oakwood.edu

* Paine College (Ga.), www.paine.edu

* Paul Quinn College (Tex.), www.pqc.edu

* Philander Smith College (Ark.), www.philander.edu

* Prairie View A&M University (Tex.), www.pvamu.edu

* Rust College (Miss.), www.rustcollege.edu

* Saint Augustine's College (N.C.), www.st-aug.edu

* Saint Paul's College (Va.), www.saintpauls.edu

* Saint Philip's College (Tex.) www.accd.edu/spc/spcmain/spc.htm

* Savannah State University (Ga.), www.savstate.edu

* Selma University (Ala.)

* Shaw University (N.C.), www.shawuniversity.edu

* Shelton State Community College (Ala.) www.sheltonstate.edu/sscc

* Shorter College (Ark.)

* South Carolina State University (S.C.), www.scsu.edu

* Southern University and A&M College, Baton Rouge (La.), www. subr.edu

* Southern University, New Orleans (La.), www.suno.edu

* Southern University, Shreveport (La.), www.susla.edu

* Southwestern Christian College (Tex.), www.swcc.edu

* Spelman College (Ga.), www.spelman.edu

* Stillman College (Ala.), www.stillman.edu

* Talladega College (Ala.), www.talladega.edu

* Tennessee State University (Tenn.), www.tnstate.edu

* Texas College (Tex.), www.texascollege.edu

* Texas Southern University (Tex.), www.tsu.edu

* Tougaloo College (Miss.), www.tougaloo.edu

* Trenholm State Technical College (Ala.) www.trenholmtech.cc.al.us

* Tuskegee University (Ala.), www.tuskegee.edu

* University of Arkansas at Pine Bluff (Ark.), www.uapb.edu

* University of Maryland, Eastern Shore (Md.), www.umes.edu

* University of the District of Columbia (D.C.), www.universityofdc.org

* University of the Virgin Islands (V.I.), www.uvi.edu

* Virginia State University (Va.), www.vsu.edu

* Virginia Union University (Va.), www.vuu.edu

* Voorhees College (S.C.), www.voorhees.edu

* West Virginia State University (W.Va.), www.wvstateu.edu

* Wilberforce University (Ohio), www.wilberforce.edu

* Wiley College (Tex.), www.wileyc.edu

* Winston-Salem State University (N.C.), www.wssu.edu

* Xavier University of Louisiana (La.), www.xula.edu

"We've got to show people the Africa that looks like them. An everyday Africa - families going home from work who live in cities, children who wear uniforms to schools and come to Harvard and Yale and outperform us. We've got to look at that part of Africa that we can find common ground with."
Randall Robinson, founder of Trans Africa

What's your African IQ?

Find out what you know by answering the following questions
1. What 2006 Academy Award-winning movie became the first mainstream motion picture to be filmed entirely on location in Uganda?
   a. Blood Diamond
   b. Babel
   c. Pirates of the Caribbean
   d. The Last King of Scotland

2. How accurate was the writer Edgar Rice Burroughs' depiction of Senegal in the novel Tarzan?
   a. Very accurate. Because of Burroughs, I want to visit the homeland.
   b. Tarzan didn't take place in Senegal. It was Nigeria!
   c. Entertaining read, but no truth to it at all.
   d. Slightly accurate, except that Tarzan took place in Brazil.

3. Ellen Johnson-Sir leaf is the first democratically elected female president of what African country?

   a. South Africa
   b. Botswana
   c. Mozambique
   d. Liberia

4. What African country is completely surrounded by South Africa?

   a. Zimbabwe
   b. Namibia
   c. Lesotho
   d. Angola

5. True or false: Africa is losing its environmentally protected big game animals to diners in Paris and London?

6. Which country has the worlds' largest supply of platinum mines?

   a. Russia
   b. Lesotho
   c. Zimbabwe
   d. South Africa

7. What African country was founded by African Americans?

   a. Congo
   b. Ethiopia
   c. Niger
   d. Liberia

8. How much money did South African singer Solomon Linda make from creating "The Lion Sleeps Tonight", the hit song featured in a Disney international hit "The Lion King"?

   a. 10 shillings
   b. $5,000
   c. Zero
   d. $2.3 million, plus rights for all future Broadway productions of "The Lion King"

9. Which of the following celebrities were not born in Africa?

   a. Chiwetel Ejiofor
   b. Djimon Hounsou
   c. Idris Elba
   d. Youssou NDour

10. Which of these cities is not in Africa?

    a. Cairo
    b. Dar Es Salaam
    c. Tripoli
    d. Pretoria
    e. Mumbai

11. Mt. Kilamanjaro is in what African country?

    a. Tanzania
    b. Kenya
    c. Uganda
    d. Ghana

12. What is the largest country in Africa?

    a. Egypt
    b. South Africa
    c. Sudan
    d. Nigeria

13. Supermodel Iman is from what African country?

    a. Ethiopia
    b. Sudan
    c. Somalia
    d. Chad

14. The Academy Award-winning film "Casablanca", starring Humphrey Bogart and Ingrid Bergman, was set in what country?
    a. Morocco
    b. Algeria
    c. Mali
    d. Sierra Leone

15. Which of the following countries is an island?

    a. Ivory Coast
    b. Madagascar
    c. Cameroon
    d. Libya

16. Darfur is the site of a brutal civil war that has claimed more than a million lives. But where in Africa is Darfur?

    a. Rwanda
    b. Sudan
    c. Congo
    d. Uganda

17. Hale Selasse I, the father of Rastafarian's, was from what country?

    a. Jamaica
    b. Somalia
    c. Ethiopia
    d. Egypt

18. Which of the following animals are not native to Africa?

    a. Gorillas
    b. Lions
    c. Elephants
    d. Tigers

19. To which country did "Roots" author Alex Haley trace his African ancestry?

    a. Ghana
    b. South Africa
    c. Gambia
    d. Ivory Coast

20. Africa is located between what two oceans?

    a. Indian Ocean
    b. Pacific Ocean
    c. Atlantic Ocean
    d. Arctic Ocean

Answer to African IQ quiz: page 300

Key events in Africa's history

1440s
The first African people are captured, taken to Portugal and enslaved. In 1514, the Atlantic slave trade begins, forcibly removing 12 million Africans and transporting them to various countries.

1832/1863
The British abolish slavery in the West Indies, and slaves in the United States are emancipated in 1863.

1850s
"The New Era" (1855) was the first privately owned newspaper established in Sierra Leone, and it was the beginning of the Black African newspaper press.

1871-1912
Global European imperialism in heightened throughout Africa and colonization cuts throughout the continent.

1884-85
The Berlin Conference convenes. Rivalries among European countries (Belgium, France, Germany, Great Britain, Italy, Spain and Portugal) and the United States, for claim to African holdings resulted in the Berlin Conference. While negotiations were made, no African states were represented at the conference.

1899-1902
The Anglo-Boer (Afrikaner) War in South Africa leads to the domination of the country's Black majority.

1947
Decolonization movements intensify after the end of World War II (1939-1945).

1948
South African literature exposes the plight of Black Africans and apartheid, a legalized system of racial separation, by writers such as Thomas Mofolo, Solomon Tshekisho, Neil Parsons and Samuel E. K. Mqhayi.

1957
Ghana becomes an independent Black state under Kwame Nkrumah. Sierra Leone (1961), Gambia (1965) and other states follow.

1954-1962
French colonies in Africa resist French rule. In 1962, after a civil war in Algeria, the country gains its independence, preceded by Morocco and Tunisia.

1950-1960s
Dennis Brutus, a South African poet and activist, describes racial oppression in South Africa in "Sirens Knuckles Boots", his poetry collection, which outlined the everyday horrors of apartheid. Other Black intellectuals and literary greats emerge, including Wole Soyinka, Cheikh Anta Diop, Ama Ata Aidoo and Ngugi wa Thiong'o.

1964
Nelson Mandela is on trial among with other members of the African National Congress (ANC) in South Africa. Mandela delivers his famous "Speech from the Dock" at the Pretoria Supreme Court before he was imprisoned on Robben Island. He spends a total of 27 years behind bars.

1970s
Portugal loses its hold on African colonies, including Angola and Mozambique.

1971
Idi Amin Dada stages a coup and becomes self-appointed head of Uganda. The following year he expels Ugandan Asians from the country.

1972
Steve Biko, born in King William's Town, South Africa, helped to found the Black People's Convention (BPC) and became the national leader of the Black Consciousness Movement. The organizations galvanized the

country's anti-apartheid movement. Biko died while in a Pretoria prison in 1977, and the brutality of this death was exposed in the national media.

1979
Idi Amin Dada is ousted from power by Tanzanian troops and Ugandan exiles.

1980s
The world is horrified as the brutality if apartheid in South Africa is exposed in the national media.

1984
The first cases of HIV and AIDS in Africa are reported in Uganda. Other states soon report findings of the disease, including Kenya and Tanzania.

1985
"Live Aid" concerts featuring celebrity performances are held at London's Wembley Stadium and the JFK Stadium in Philadelphia. The concerts raised millions of dollars for famine relief in Africa.

1990
Nelson Mandela is freed.

1993
Nelson Mandela and South African President F.W. de Klerk are awarded the Nobel Peace Prize.

1994
South Africa holds its first multiracial elections in April and Nelson Mandela is elected the country's president. In central Africa, the Hutus massacre as many as 1 million Tutsis in Rwanda. Fearing reprisals, about 1 million Hutus fled Rwanda to Zaire and Tanzania during a much-publicized exodus.

2003
Darfur conflict in Sudan begins between two groups - the Sudanese government and rebel groups (the Sudan Liberation Movement and the Justice and Equality Movement). More than 400.000 die in the conflict and 2 million civilian refugees remain in danger.

2005
Ellen Johnson-Sirleaf becomes Africa's first female elected head of state following Liberia's presidential race.

2006
An estimated 25 million Africans are infected with the HIV virus.

2007
Foreign ministers of China and Africa launch their first annual talks in October as Beijing continues to expand its footprint in the resource-rich continent. "China and Africa are good friends, close partners and dear brothers," Chinese Foreign Minister Yang Jiechi said as he shook hands and welcomed a long line of his African counterparts to the meeting at the UN.

2008
Barack Obama is elected first African American President in the United States.

Answers to African IQ quiz:
1. D. "The Last King of Scotland"
2. C. Burroughs was rumored to have never visited Africa.
3. D. She was elected in 2005.
4. C. Lesotho
5. True. The "African Journal of Ecology" says European dinner palates play a part in killing kob antilopes.
6. D. South Africa has 85 percent of the world's platinum reserves.
7. D. Liberia
8. A. Solomon Linda wrote the 1939 song, originally titled "Mbube" (or lion in Zulu) and licensed it for 10 shillings to a South African label. He died in 1962, his family poor and destitute. But the Linda family launched a copyright lawsuit, and in 2006 won $1.6 million in royalties.
9. A and C. Actors Idris Elba and Chiwetel Ejiofor were born in England. Elbe is of West African decent, and Ejiofor is of Nigerian descent. Hounsou is an actor originally from Benin. NDour is a pre-eminent Senegalese.
10. E. Mumbai is in India.
11. A. Tanzania
12. C. Sudan
13. C. Somalia
14. A. Morocco
15. B. Madagascar
16. B. Sudan
17. C. Ethiopia
18. D. Tigers are native to Asia, but a new program releases Chinese Tigers into Africa to help the rare animals increase in population.
19. C. Gambia
20. A and C.

Scoring your African IQ
If you got ...
-17 to 20 answers right, congratulations! You've got the basics down pat!
-12 to 16 answers right, good try.
-9 to 12 answers right, time to pay more attention to news from Africa.
-4 to 9 answers right, better hit the library.
-0 to 4 answers correct, consider hiring a tutor, or learn more about Africa in this and future issues of ebony magazine.

Why we celebrate - or don't celebrate Kwanzaa

For many African-Americans post-Christmas holiday is filled with joy, confusion and ambivalence

By Shirley Henderson

Kwanzaa, the seven-day afro centric spiritual festival, turns 43 in December of 2009. Since its inception by founder Maulana Karenga in 1966, many faithful celebrants have lit the kinara while espousing the Nguzo saba (Seven principles) of Kwanzaa.

On the other side of the kente cloth is a decidedly anti-Kwanzaa group that does not participate in the celebration for reasons that range from unfavorable Karenga sentiment to the festival's growing commercialism.

And there are those who are ambivalent about Kwanzaa and still others who don't understand the holiday.

Like many steadfast Kwanzaa celebrants, Soyini Walton recalls discovering herself culturally in the 1960s while she was in her 20s. "We were inspired to do that by the cry of the Stokely Carmichael," recalls Walton, principal of Barbara Sizemore Academy in Chicago and one of the founders of the Institute for positive Education. Both schools incorporate many of the principles of Kwanzaa into their curriculum. "Carmichael stood up, raised his fist and said, 'Black Power,' and that was kind of a cultural awakening... People coming out of the Civil Rights Movement were very active, and they were frustrated just simply doing civil rights. They wanted to do something that was reflective of our background... and our own power."

When Karenga created Kwanzaa, which is ripe with ceremony and culture - lighting candles, singing songs, reaffirming dedication to the seven principles with Swahili names and enjoying the karamu (feast) - many people embraced its doctrine. Initially Kwanzaa celebrations were held in private homes on each day of the festival to correspond with the seven principles: umoja (unity), kujichagulia (self-determination), ujima (collective work and responsibility), ujamaa (cooperative economics), nia (purpose), kuumba (creativity) and imani (faith). Today, in major cities across the country, Kwanzaa celebrations are held at such locations as colleges, convention halls and community centers.

Maitefa Angaza of Brooklyn loves the idea of the spiritual festival. A mother and grandmother, she has been actively celebrating Kwanzaa for three decades, and she decided to write a guide to help others embrace the festival. Kwanzaa: From Holiday To Everyday (Kensington Publishing Corp.) outlines how she and her family prepare for and celebrate the festival, which begins December 26 and ends on January 1.

"One thing that I've found personally gratifying because I've been celebrating Kwanzaa for 30 years, " says Angaza, "is that my son who turns 30, used to enjoy lighting the candles and putting a piece of fruit on the table. Now he's doing the same things with his child."

Despite its ceremonial aspects, Kwanzaa is considered to be a non-religious celebration. Still, there are some, such as Carlotta Morrow, who believe that celebrating Kwanzaa encroaches upon religion by teaching people to live their lives according to certain doctrine.

Morrow, a San Diego-based writer, says that during the 1970s, her sister became involved with Organization US, started by Karenga. After taking a Swahili name, her sister denounced Christianity. Morrow and her family were alarmed, and she decided to attend one of the group's meetings. Not liking what she heard, she began researching the organization and its founder. Ten years ago, Morrow decided to warn others about what she perceived to be strong anti-Christian sentiments connected to Karenga's teachings. She put up an anti-Kwanzaa Web Site called The Truth About Kwanzaa (www.christocentric.com/Kwanzaa/). "I put some excerpts from [Karenga's] books in my Web site so that people could see that he created Kwanzaa as an alternative to the Christmas season," says Morrow. (Karenga could not be reached for comment.)

She believes that Kwanzaa has spiritualized Black History, especially when its rituals are practiced inside churches. "When you use Black History to make changes socially, then it becomes a religion," Morrow insists. "In other words, we have all the principles that we need to become a better man, woman or child in our Bible. We don't need anything else. It's blasphemy that people are mixing Biblical principles with Kwanzaa principles."

According to the official Kwanzaa Web site (www.officialkwanzaawebsite. org/index.shtml), more than 20 million people worldwide celebrate the festival and many of them are Christians. Those who participate in the holiday do not see a conflict for Christians or any other religious group that my choose to participate in Kwanzaa ceremonies. "We don't call Valentine's Day a pagan holiday," says Walton. "[Kwanzaa] is about the culture - not only the history of African-Americans and African people, but also of our future. Each of the seven days gives us instructions on how to care for self and our communities."

Could Kwanzaa and its principles offer a way to instill unity and pride into the Black race? Even if Kwanzaa's sole purpose is to institute positive change in the Black community, there are still skeptics who question whether it meets that goal. Gregory Sain is a Chicago-based motivational speaker and radio personality who became a Muslim in 1983. He says that like many holidays Kwanzaa has become a commercialized celebration that has lost its original meaning.

Now a member of a Christian church, Sain says that he believes in the principles of Kwanzaa but rarely see them exhibited, even among Christians who practice it. "We don't live anything close to what goes on with Kwanzaa," he says. "Nor do we [live it] in churches where you are supposed to love your neighbor. In Black neighborhoods, the people don't even come out of the house. Is it fear? What is really going on?"

About Kwanzaa
-Founded: 1966
-Purpose: The non-religious holiday celebrates family, community and culture, and reaffirms values of African culture
-Observed: December 26 - January 1

Great Days in Harlem

The birth of the Harlem Renaissance

by Beth Rowen & Borgna Brunner

Originally called the New Negro Movement, the Harlem Renaissance was a literary and intellectual flowering that fostered a new black cultural identity in the 1920s and 1930s. Critic and teacher Alain Locke described it as a "spiritual coming of age" in which the black community was able to seize upon its "first chances for group expression and self determination."

With racism still rampant and economic opportunities scarce, creative expression was one of the few avenues available to African Americans in the early twentieth century. Chiefly literary—the birth of jazz is generally considered a separate movement—the Harlem Renaissance, according to Locke, transformed "social disillusionment to race pride."

Perfect Timing

The timing of this coming-of-age was perfect. The years between World War I and the Great Depression were boom times for the United States, and jobs were plentiful in cities, especially in the North. Between 1920 and 1930, almost 750,000 African Americans left the South, and many of them migrated to urban areas in the North to take advantage of the prosperity—and the more racially tolerant environment. The Harlem section of Manhattan, which covers just 3 sq mi, drew nearly 175,000 African Americans, turning the neighborhood into the largest concentration of black people in the world.

Literary Roots

Black-owned magazines and newspapers flourished, freeing African Americans from the constricting influences of mainstream white society. Charles S. Johnson's Opportunity magazine became the leading voice of black culture, and W.E.B. DuBois's journal, The Crisis, with Jessie Redmon Fauset as its literary editor, launched the literary careers of such writers as Arna Bontemps, Langston Hughes, and Countee Cullen.

Other luminaries of the period included writers Zora Neale Hurston, Claude McKay, Jean Toomer, Rudolf Fisher, Wallace Thurman, and Nella Larsen. The movement was in part given definition by two anthologies: James Weldon Johnson's The Book of American Negro Poetry and Alain Locke's The New Negro.

"Our Individual Dark-Skinned Selves"

The white literary establishment soon became fascinated with the writers of the Harlem Renaissance and began publishing them in larger numbers. But for the writers themselves, acceptance by the white world was less important, as Langston Hughes put it, than the "expression of our individual dark-skinned selves."

The Short list of Black Inventions and Patents.

This information was gathered from a number of sources (web sites, newspapers, magazines and text books), including "Introduction to African Civilizations" by John G. Jackson, "Africa Before They Came" by Galbraith Welch, "The River" by Edward Hooper, "Fordham University's Internet African History Sourcebook" and BBC News Online, Civilizations Past & Present... by Robert R. Edgar (Author), Neil J. Hackett (Author), George F. Jewsbury (Author), Barbara S. Molony (Author), Matthew Gordon (Author)

THE SHORT LIST OF BLACK INVENTIONS AND PATENTS

the original Traveling exhibit OF Black inventors and Scientists Paper (Papyrus)

Ancient Egypt (Khemet)Alphabet (Hieroglyphics) Ancient Egypt (Khemet) STETHOSCOPE Ancient Egypt Imhotep 3rd Dynasty

Electric Lamp Lewis H. Latimer & Joseph V. Nichols TYPE WRITING MACHINE

Lee S. Burridge & Newman R. Marshman BICYCLE FRAME

Isaac R. Johnson LANTER

Michael C. Harney HAND STAMP

William B. Purvis LETTER (Mail) BOX

Philip B. Downing KEY (Chain) FASTENER

Fredrick J. Loudin PENCIL SHARPENER

John Lee Love HORSESHOE

Oscar E. Brown RIDING (Horse) SADDLE

William D. Davis THERMOSTATIC CONTROLLED HAIR CURLERS, COMBS & IRONS

Solomon Harper REFRIGERATOR

John Stanard RANGES (Gas Stove)

Thomas A. Carrington CLOTHES DRIER (Dryer)

George T. Sampson EGG BEATER

Willis Johnson MOP Thomas W. Stewart DUST PAN

Lloyd P. Ray GOLF TEE

George F. Grant HEATING FURNACE

Alice H. Parker STAINLESS STEEL SCOURING PADS

Alfred Benjamin Gamma Electric Cell

Henry T. Sampson FIRE EXTINGUISHER

Thomas J. Martin IRONING BOARD

Sarah Boone PHONOGRAPH

Joseph Hunter Dickinson TELEPHONE TRANSMITTER

Granville T. Woods FOLDING CHAIR

Charles Randolph Beckley FOLDING BED

Leonard C. Bailey GUITAR

Robert F. Flemings, Jr. HYDRAULIC SHOCK ABSORBER

Ralph W. Sanderson LAWN MOWER

John Albert Burr AUTOMATIC (Transmission) GEAR SHIFT

Richard B. Spikes TRAFFIC SIGNAL

Garrett A. Morgan EYE PROTECTOR (Safety Goggles)

Powell Johnson AIR CONDITIONING UNIT

Frederick M. Jones PROGRAMMABLE TV RECEIVER (Remote) CONTROLLERS

Joseph N. Jackson FOUNTAIN PEN

William B. Purvis DISPOSABLE SYRINGE

Phil Brooks URINALYSIS MACHINE

Dewey S.C. Sanderson ELEVATOR

Alexander Miles CARBON DIOXIDE LASER FUELS

Lester A. Lee & Edward E. Baroody OIL CUP (Lubricator Cup)

Elijah McCoy Source of the phrase: ("The Real McCoy") PHI-ANO (THE ROYEL) Royel "Future Man" Wooten CURTAIN ROD

Samuel R. Scottron TWO-CYCLE GAS ENGINE

Frederick M. Jones BRAID SINGEING CLAMP

Vera A. Jarrett (Hott Scizzors) DOOR (Knob) HOLDING DEVICE

Osbourn Dorsey CHAMBER COMMODE (Toilet)

Thomas Elkins APPARATUS FOR ABLATING AND REMOVING CATARACT LENSES

Dr. Patricia E. Bath BREATHING DEVICE (Gas Mask)

Garrett A. Morgan STREET SWEEPER

Charles B. Brooks CHILD'S (Baby) CARRIAGE

William H. Richardson WEIGHT LIFTING BAR APPARATUS (For NFL)

Jesse Hoagland WRENCH

John Arthur Johnson UTILITY CARRIER (Wheel-It)

Joseph Edmonds BRUSH (Hair)

Lyda D. Newman COMB

Walter H. Sammon DOUBLE TANK PINCH TRIGGER PUMP WATER GUN (Super Soaker)

Lonnie G. Johnson & Bruce M. D'Andrade ENVELOP SEAL

Frank W. Leslie COIN CHANGER MECHANISM

James A. Bauer MORTICIAN'S TABLE

Leander M. Coles HOME SECURITY SYSTEM utilizing TV Surveillance

Marie Van Brittan Brown & Albert L. Brown
AIR SHIP ("The Blimp")
John F. Pickering PROPELLING MEANS FOR AEROPLANES
James Sloan Adams HELICOPTER
Paul E. Williams FLYING LANDING PLATFORM
Peachy Booker LASTING (Shoe Making) MACHINE
Jan Earnst Matzeliger SEED PLANTER
Henry Blair COTTON PLANTER
Henry Blair AUTOMATIC FISHING (Reel) DEVICE
George Cook CAR COUPLING (Automatic Train Hitch)
Andrew Jackson Beard INSECT DESTROYER
Albert C. Richardson
TO BE CONTINUED....
BY THE PRESENT GENERATIONS.....

1721	Onesimes	Developed a cure for the smallpox virus.
1752	Benjamin Banneker	

         * created the first clock ever built in the United States

         * first Black Presidential appointee

         * developed the layout for the streets and monuments for the nation's capitol, Washington, D.C., including the White House, Capitol building and Treasury building

1821	Thomas L. Jennings	Receives a patent for a dry-cleaning process. Is the first patent issued to a Black person.
1834	Henry Blair	Receives a patent for a corn-planting machine.
1836	Henry Blair	Receives a patent for a cotton-planting machine.
1843	Norbert Rillieux	Developed a method for refining sugar. It consisted of a series of vacuum pans combined in a step-by-step process to make heated evaporated sugar into crystallized granules.

1848	Lewis Temple	Developed the Toggle Harpoon.
1850	James Forten	Developed a control for Ship Sails.
1853	Elfe	Was a slave and pharmacist in South Caroline. According to some accounts, he kept a prescription book, last dated 1853, in which he outlined several drugs he created. Apparently, Elfe also sold his concoctions, though little is known about those creations.
1858	Sarah E. Goode	Received a patent for her design of a folding cabinet bed, the predecessor of the sofabed.
1867	H. Lee	Received a patent for an animal trap.
	W. A. Deitz	Received a patent for a shoe design.
1870	T. Elkins	Received a patent for a combination dining/ironing table/quilting frame.
	J. W. West	Received a patent for a wagon design
	H. Spears	Received a patent for a portable shield for infantry personnel.
1871	L. Bell	Received a patent for a train smokestack.
1872	T. Elkins	Received a patent for a chamber commode.
	T. J. Byrd	Received a patent for horse reins.
	T. J. Byrd	Received a patent for a horse and carriage device.
	T. J. Byrd	Received a patent for a horse yoke design.
	T. J. Marshall	Received a patent for a fire extinguisher design.
1872	Elijah McCoy	Acquired his first patent for his invention of an automatic lubricating device, allowing a moving steam engine to be lubricated without having to first stop it.
	L. Bell	Received a patent for a dough kneader.
1873	Elijah McCoy	Received a second patent for a modification of automatic lubricating device.
1874	Lewis Howard Latimer and Brown	Received a patent for an improved of a train water closet, a bathroom compartment for railroad trains.

	E. H. Hutton	Received a patent for a cotton cultivator.
	Elijah McCoy	Received a patent for a ironing table.
	H. Pickett	Received a patent for a scaffold design.
	T. J. Byrd	Received a patent for a train coupling design.
1875	D. A. Fisher	Received a patent for a joiners' clamp.
	A. P. Ashborne	Receives a patent for a process for preparation of coconut oil.
	H. H. Nash	Received a patent for a life preserving stool.
	A. P. Ashborne	Received a patent for a biscuit cutter.
1876	D. A. Fisher	Received a patent for a furniture castor.
	T. A. Carrington	Received a patent for a range.
1877	A. P. Ashborne	Received a patent for a process for treatment of coconut oil.
1878	B. H. Taylor	Received a patent for a rotary design engine.
	J. R. Winters	Received a patent for a fire escape ladder.
	W. R. Davis, Jr.	Received a patent for a library table.
	W. A. Lavalette	Received a patent for a variation on the printing press.
	O. Dorsey	Received a patent for a door-handling device.
1879	M. W. Binga	Received a patent for a street-sprinkling apparatus.
	William Bailes	Received a patent for a ladder scaffolding support system.
	T. Elkins	Received a patent for a refrigerating device.
1880	S. R. Scottron	Received a patent for an adjustable window cornice.
	J. N. Waller	Received a patent for a shoemaker's cabinet.
	A. P. Ashbourne	Received a patent for a coconut oil refining process.
	T. B. Pinn	Received a patent for a file holder design.
	P. Johnson	Received a patent for an eye protector.
1881	J. Wormley	Received a patent for a lifesaving apparatus.

	W. S. Campbell	Received a patent for a self-setting animal trap.
	Lewis Howard Latimer and Joseph V. Nichols	Received a patent for their invention of an improvement of the incandescent light bulb with a carbon filament.
	P. Johnson	Received a patent for a swinging chairs designs.
1882	Lewis Howard Latimer and Tregoning	Received a patent for a globe support for an electric lamp.
	E. Little	Received a patent for a bridle bit design.
	A. C. Richardson	Received a patent for a hame fastener.
	W. B. Purvis	Received a patent for a bag fastener.
	Lewis Howard Latimer	Received a patent for manufacturing carbons.
1883	S. R. Scottron	Received a patent for a cornice.
	W. B. Purvis	Received a patent for a hand stamp.
	H. H. Reynolds	Received a patent for a railway window ventilator.
	J. Cooper	Received a patent for a shutter and fastening device.
	W. Washington	Received a patent for a corn-husking machine.
	L. C. Bailey	Received a patent for a combination truss and bandage.
	S. E. Thomas	Received a patent for a waste trap.
1884	C. L. Mitchell	Received a patent for a phneterisin.
	W. Johnson	Received a patent for an eggbeater.
	L. Blue	Received a patent for a corn-shelling device.
	Granville Woods	Received a patent for a steam boiler.
	T. S. Church	Received a patent for a carpet-beating machine.
	J. W. Reed	Received a patent for a dough kneader and roller.
	Granville Woods	Received a patent for a telephone transmitter.

	John P. Parker	Received a patent for a tobacco press and screw.
1885	G. T. Sampson	Received a patent for a sled propeller.
	W. F. Cosgrove	Received a patent for an automatic stop plug for gas oil pipes.
	Granville Woods	Received a patent for an apparatus for transmitting messages by electricity.
	Elijah McCoy	Received a patent for a steam dome.
	Sarah Goode	Receives a patent for a folding cabinet bed.
	W. C. Carter	Received a patent for an umbrella stand.
1886	Lewis Howard Latimer	Received a patent for an apparatus for disinfecting and cooling.
	R. F. Fleming, Jr.	Received a patent for a guitar design.
	J. Ricks	Received a patent for a horseshoe design.
	W. Marshall	Received a patent for a grain binder.
	W. H. Richardson	Received a patent for a cotton chopper.
	W. D. Davis	Received a patent for a riding saddle.
	M. Headen	Received a patent for a foot power hammer.
	Henry Brown	Received a patent for a paper storer.
	I. D. Davis	Received a patent for a tonic.
	J. Robinson	Received a patent for a dinner pail.
	Jan Matzeliger	Received a patent for his Lasting Machine which revolutionized the shoe industry.
1887	E. W. Stewart	Received a patent for a machine for making vehicle seat bars.
	J. Gregory	Received a patent for a motor design.
	Elijah McCoy	Received a patent for a lubricator attachment.
	E. R. Lewis	Received a patent for a spring gun.
	Elijah McCoy	Received a patent for a safety valve lubricator.
	D. W. Shorter	Received a patent for a feed rack.
	E. W. Stewart	Received a patent for a punching machine.
	Granville T. Woods	Received a patent for a relay instrument.
	Granville T. Woods	Received a patent for a polarized relay.

	Granville T. Woods	Received a patent for a electromechanical brake.
	R. Hawkins	Received a patent for a harness attachment.
	A. Miles	Received a patent for an elevator concept.
	Granville T. Woods	Received a patent for a phone system and apparatus.
	Granville T. Woods	Received a patent for a railway signal.
	Granville T. Woods	Received a patent for an induction telegraph system.
	Stewart and Johnson	Received a patent for a metal bending machine.
1888	A. B. Blackburn	Received a patent for a railway signal.
	D. Johnson	Received a patent for a rotary dining table.
	A. B. Blackburn	Received a patent for a spring seat for chairs.
	M. A. Cherry	Received a patent for a velocipede design.
	Granville T. Woods	Received a patent for an overhead conducting system for electric trains.
	Granville T. Woods	Received a patent for an electromotive train system.
	Miriam Benjamin	Received a patent for a Gong and Signal Chair that could be used in hotels and restaurants. It worked by pressing a small button on the back of a chair which would relay a signal to a waiting attendant. At the same time a light would illuminate on the chair allowing the attendant to see which guest was in need of assistance.
	Granville T. Woods	Received a patent for a galvanic battery.
	A. B. Blackburn	Received a patent for a cash carrier.
	O. B. Claire	Received a patent for a trestle design.
	P. W. Cornwall	Received a patent for a draft regulator.
	S. E. Thomas	Received a patent for a pipe connection design.
	J. S. Coolidge	Received a patent for a harness attachment.

	R. N. Hyde	Received a patent for a carpet cleaner formula.
	H. Creamer	Received a patent for a steam trap feeder.
	W. A. Johnson	Received a patent for a paint vehicle.
	Frank Winn	Received a patent for a direct acting steam engine.
1889	Granville T. Woods	Received a patent for an automatic safety cutout for electric circuit.
	H. Peterson	Received a patent for a lawn mower attachment.
	A. Romain	Received a patent for a passenger register.
	Purdy and Sadgwar	Received a patent for a folding chair design.
	W. H. Richardson	Received a patent for a child's carriage.
	W. A. Martin	Received a patent for a lock design.
	D. Johnson	Received a patent for a lawn mower attachment.
	J. Standard	Received a patent for an oil stove design.
	Elijah McCoy and Hodges	Received a patent for a lubricating device.
1890	W. B. Purvis	Received a patent for a fountain pen.
	F. J. Ferrell	Received a patent for a steam trap.
	Jan Matzeliger	Received a patent for a tack-separating mechanism.
	H. Faulkner	Received a patent for a ventilated shoe.
	F. J. Ferrell	Received a patent for a snow-melting device.
	P. B. Downing	Received a patent for an electric railroad switch.
	D. Johnson	Received a patent for a lawn mower grass catcher.
	A. Pugsley	Received a patent for a blind stop.
	A. F. Hilyer	Received a patent for a water evaporator attachment for hot-air register.
	J. W. Benton	Received a patent for a derrick for hoisting.

	H. H. Reynolds	Received a patent for a safety gate for bridges.
	Snow and Johns	Received a patent for a liniment formula.
	Isaac Watkins	Received a patent for a scrubbing frame.
	D. McCree	Received a patent for a portable fire escape.
1891	Daniel Hale Williams	Opens Provident Hospital in Chicago, which includes a school to train black doctors and nurses.
	W. Murray	Received a patent for an attachment for bicycles.
	P. D. Smith	Received a patent for a potato digger.
	A. C. Richardson	Received a patent for a churn design.
	W. B. Abrams	Received a patent for a hame attachment.
	G. Toliver	Received a patent for a propeller design.
	J. Standard	Received a patent for a refrigerator design.
	W. Queen	Received a patent for a guard for companionways and hatches.
	H. Linden	Received a patent for a piano truck.
	Jan Matzeliger	Received a patent for improvements to his shoe lasting machine.
	Elijah McCoy	Received a patent for a oil drip cup.
	P. B. Downing	Received a patent for a letter box design.
	Granville T. Woods	Received a patent for an electric railway system.
1892	Henry A. Bowman	Received a patent for a flag-making technique.
	F. R. Perryman	Received a patent for a caterer's tray table.
	P. D. Smith	Received a patent for a grain binder.
	C. Williams	Received a patent for a canopy frame.
	Sarah Boone	Came up with an idea for a narrow wooden board, with collapsible leg supports and covered with padding. Prior to her ironing board, this task normally required taking a plank and placing it between two chairs or simply using the dining table.

	R. Coates	Received a patent for an overboot design for horses.
	G. T. Sampson	Received a patent for a clothes dryer.
	Andrew Beard	Received a patent for as rotary engine.
	O. E. Brown	Received a patent for a horseshoe design.
	S. R. Scottron	Received a patent for a curtain rod.
	A. L. Lewis	Received a patent for a window cleaner.
	G. E. Becket	Received a patent for a letter box design.
	L. F. Brown	Received a patent for a bridle bit.
	F. J. Loudin	Received a patent for a sash fastener.
1893	Daniel Hale Williams	Was the first doctor in the world to perform a successful open-heart operation.
	P. W. Cornwall	Received a patent for a draft regulator.
	J. R. Watts	Received a patent for a bracket for miners' lamps.
	L. W. Benjamin	Received a patent for a broom moistener and bridle.
	T. W. Stewart	Received a patent for the mop.
	T. W. Stewart	Received a patent for a station indicator.
	E. R. Robinson	Received a patent for an electronic trolley design.
	C. B. Brooks	Received a patent for a punch.
1894	F. J. Loudin	Received a patent for a key fastener.
	George Washington Murray	Received a patent for a furrow opener/stalk knocker.
	George Washington Murray	Received a patent for a cultivator and marker.
	S. Newson	Received a patent for an oil heater and cooker.
	George Washington Murray	Received a patent for a planter design.
	George Washington Murray	Received a patent for a cotton chopper.
	George Washington Murray	Received a patent for a fertilizer distributor.

	George Washington Murray	Received a patent for a combined cotton seed.
	R. H Gray	Received a patent for a bailing press.
	Joseph Lee	Received a patent for a bread-kneading machine.
	A. C. Richardson	Received a patent for a casket-lowering device.
1895	M. A. Cherry	Received a patent for a streetcar fender.
	J. T. Dawkins	Received a patent for a ventilation aid.
	H. Creamer	Received a patent for a steam feed water trap design.
	C. J. Dorticus	Received a patent for a shoe-drying device.
	J. Cooper	Received a patent for a elevator device.
	C. J. Dorticus	Received a patent for a photo print wash.
	C. J. Dorticus	Received a patent for a photo embossing machine.
	R. H. Gray	Received a patent for a cistern cleaners.
	Purdy and Peters	Received a patent for a spoon design.
	W. B. Purvis	Received a patent for a magnetic car-balancing device.
	Joseph Lee	Received a patent for a bread-crumbling machine.
	J. L. Love	Received a patent for a plasterers' hawk.
	L. A. Russell	Received a patent for a guard attachment for a bed.
	E. H. Holmes	Received a patent for a gauge design.
	J. B. Allen	Received a patent for a clothesline support.
1896	W. D. Davis	Received a patent for a riding saddle.
	H. Grenon	Received a patent for a razor stropping device.
	William H. Johnson	Received a patent for overcoming dead centers.
	Jan Matzeliger	Received a patent for a shoe-nailing machine.
	C. B. Brooks	Received a patent for a street sweeper.

	Lewis Howard Latimer	Received a patent for a locking coat and hat rack.
	D. N. Roster	Received a patent for a feather curler.
	A. J. Polk	Received a patent for a bicycle support.
	W. S. Grant	Received a patent for a curtain rod support.
	O'Conner and Turner	Received a patent for an alarm for boilers.
	O'Conner and Turner	Received a patent for a steam gauge design.
	H. A. Jackson	Received a patent for a kitchen table design.
	K. Morehead	Received a patent for a reel carrier.
	W. Purdy	Received a patent for a tool sharpener.
	Granville T. Woods	Received a patent for an electricity distribution system.
	J. H Hunter	Received a patent for a portable weighing scale.
	J. F. Hammonds	Received a patent for a yarn holder device.
	J. T. White	Received a patent for a lemon squeezer.
1897	D. L. White	Received a patent for car extensions steps.
	A. L. Cralle	Received a patent for an ice cream mold.
	P. Walker	Received a patent for a machine for cleaning seed cotton.
	J. H. Dunnington	Received a patent for horse detachers.
	W. H. Jackson	Received a patent for a railway switch design.
	W. U. Moody	Received a patent for a game board design.
	W. H. Phelps	Received a patent for a vehicle washing apparatus.
	J. W. Smith	Received a patent for a lawn sprinkler design.
	R. A. Butler	Received a patent for a train alarm.
	C. V. Richey	Received a patent for a car-coupling design.
	T. H. Edmonds	Received a patent for a separating screen.

	B. H. Taylor	Received a patent for a slide valve.
	W. B. Purvis	Received a patent for an electric railway switch.
	L. P. Ray	Received a patent for a dust pan.
	C. V. Richey	Received a patent for a railway switch design.
	J. H. Haines	Received a patent for a portable basin.
	F. W. Leslie	Received a patent for an envelope seal design.
	J. H. Evans	Received a patent for a convertible settee.
	Andrew J. Beard	Invents the "Jenny Coupler," an automatic system for coupling railroad cars.
	J. L. Love	Received a patent for a pencil sharpener.
	E. R. Robinson	Received a patent for a casting composite.
	J. A. Sweeting	Received a patent for a cigarette-rolling device.
	C. V. Richey	Received a patent for a fire escape bracket.
1898	R. Hearness	Received a patent for a bottle cap design.
	A. L. Rickman	Received a patent for an overshoe.
	W. J. Ballow	Received a patent for a combined coatrack/table.
	Benjamin F. Jackson	Received a patent for a heating apparatus.
	P. Walker	Received a patent for a bait holder.
	J. A. Joyce	Received a patent for an ore bucket.
	Benjamin F. Jackson	Received a patent for a matrix drying apparatus.
	A. L. Ross	Received a patent for a bag closure.
	J. A. Sweeting	Received a patent for a knife/scoop design.
	G. A. E. Barnes	Received a patent for a sign design.
	W. H. Jackson	Received a patent for an automatic locking switch.
	Jones and Long	Received a patent for a bottle cap.
	C. O. Bailiff	Received a patent for a shampoo headrest.
	C. W. Allen	Received a patent for a self-leveling table.

	F. H. Harding	Received a patent for an extension banquet table.
	Elijah McCoy	Received a patent for an oil cup.
	L. D. Newman	Received a patent for a brush design.
	J. W. Outlaw	Received a patent for a horseshoe design.
	C. V. Richey	Received a patent for a hammock-stretcher.
1899	J. H. Dickenson	Received a patent for a pianola.
	E. P. Ray	Received a patent for a chair supporting device.
	A. C. Richardson	Received a patent for an insect destroyer.
	L. F. Booker	Received a patent for a rubber scraping device.
	J. H. Robinson	Received a patent for a train safety guard.
	Benjamin F. Jackson	Received a patent for a gas burner.
	J. A. Burr	Received a patent for a lawn mower.
	G. Cook	Received a patent for an automatic fishing device.
	R. R. Reynolds	Received a patent for a nonrefillable bottle.
	F. W. Griffin	Received a patent for a pool table attachment.
	W. Johnson	Received a patent for a velocipede design.
	W. J. Nickerson	Received a patent for a mandolin and guitar attachment for pianos.
	J. Ricks	Received a patent for an overshoe for horses.
	L. C. Bailey	Received a patent for a folding bed.
	B. F. Cargill	Received a patent for an invalid cot.
	C. J. Dorticus	Received a patent for a hose leak stopper.
	R. Hearness	Received a patent for a detachable car fender.
	A. R. Cooper	Received a patent for a shoemakers jack.
	Elijah McCoy	Received a patent for a lawn sprinkler system.
	J. Ross	Received a patent for a baling press.
	E. H. West	Received a patent for a weather shield.

	W. F. Burr	Received a patent for a railway switching device.
	J. W. Butts	Received a patent for a luggage carrier.
	I. R. Johnson	Received a patent for a bicycle frame.
	J. P. Williams	Received a patent for a pillow sham holder.
	W. Burwell	Received a patent for a boot or shoe.
	Jan Matzeliger	Received a patent for a tack-distributing system.
	A. Mendenhall	Received a patent for a holder for driving reins.
	A. L. Ross	Received a patent for a trousers support.
	George Grant	Received a patent for a golf tee.
	J. M. Certain	Received a patent for a parcel carrier for bicycles.
	J. B. Rhodes	Received a patent for a water closet design.
	A. C. Richardson	Received a patent for a bottle design.
1900	S. W. Gunn	Received a patent for a boot or shoe design.
	J. M. Mitchell	Received a patent for a corn planter design.
	J. F. Pickering	Received a patent for an airship.
	Madame C. J. Walker	Received a patent for a hot comb.
1901	Granville T. Woods	Received a patent for a regulating and controlling electrical translating devices.
1902	Granville T. Woods	Received a patent for an automatic air brake.
1905	Lewis Howard Latimer	Received a patent for a book support.
1910	Richard B. Spikes	Received a patent for a locking billiard cue.
	Lewis Howard Latimer	Received a patent for a lamp fixture.
1912	Frederick M. Johnson	Received a patent for a self-feeding rapid-fire rifle.

	Ernest Everett Just	Appointed head of Howard's biology department.
1914	Garrett A. Morgan	Received a patent for a gas mask.
1921	Hubert Julian	Received a patent for an airplane safety device.
1923	Garrett A. Morgan	Inventor of the gas mask, receives the patent on November 20 for the automatic traffic light, which he sells to General electric for $40,000.
1925	William Hale	Received a patent for an airplane improvement.
1926	Richard. B. Spikes	Received a patent for a milk bottle cover/opener.
1928	Marjorie Joyner	Received a patent for a hair wave machine.
1930	Solomon Harper	Received a patent for a electric hair treatment.
1931	Percy Julian	Received a patent for a physostigmine, a drug for the treatment of the eye disease glaucoma.
	Richard. B. Spikes	Received a patent for a method and apparatus for obtaining average samples and temperature of tank liquids.
1932	Richard. B. Spikes	Received a patent for an automatic gear shift design.
1938	Lloyd Hall	Received a patent for a method for sterilizing foodstuff.
1939	Richard. B. Spikes	Received a patent for an automatic shoe shine chair.
	Frederick M. Jones	Received a patent for a movie ticket-dispensing machine.
1940	Richard. B. Spikes	Received a patent for a multiple-barrel machine gun.
	Percy Julian	Received a patent for a method for recovery of sterol.
1941	Charles R. Drew	

After having established a pioneer blood bank operation at New York City Presbyterian Hospital, is named professor of surgery at Howard University. He establishes donor banks in many states to collect blood for the U.S. Armed Forces.

1942	Joseph Blair	Received a patent for a speedboat design.
1949	Lloyd Hall	Received a patent for a puncture-sealing mixture.
	Joseph Blair	Received a patent for a aerial torpedo design.
1945	Frederick M. Jones	Received a patent for a two-cycle engine.
1949	Lloyd Hall	Received a patent for a preserving process.
	Frederick M. Jones	Received a patent for an air conditioning design.
	Frederick M. Jones	Received a patent for a starter generator for cooling gas engines.
1950	Frederick M. Jones	Received a patent for a rotary compressor.
	Frederick M. Jones	Received a patent for a refrigeration unit design.
	Frederick M. Jones	Received a patent for a two-cycle gasoline engine.
	Frederick M. Jones	Received a patent for a refrigeration construction design.
1951	G. S. Bluford Sr.	Received a patent for an artillery ammunition training round.
1953	Solomon Harper	Received a patent for a thermostatic control hair curlers.
1954	Frederick M. Jones	Received a patent for a defrosting method.
	Percy Julian	Received a patent for a preparation of cortisone.
	Frederick M. Jones	Received a patent for an air-conditioning method.
1958	Frederick M. Jones	Received a patent for a combustion-engine device.
1960	Robert Bundy	Received a patent for a signal generator design.
	Frederick M. Jones	Received a patent for a thermostat design.

1966	Betsy Ancker Johnson	Received a patent for a signal generator design.
1968	Paul Brown	Received a patent for a "Wiz-z-zer" spinning top toy.
1969	M. C. Gourdine	Received a patent for an electrogas dynamic apparatus.
	George R. Carruthers	Received a patent for an ultraviolet spectrograph.
1971	Bayliss and Emrick	Received a patent for an encapsulation process.
1972	Earl Shaw	Received a patent for a spin fly tunable laser.
1973	Al Prather	Received a patent for a man-powered glider aircraft.
1978	Christian Reeburg	Received a patent for a grease gun stand.
1980	Levi Watkins, Jr.	First surgeon to implant an automatic defibrillator in the human heart, a device that corrects arrhythmia, or a failure of the heart to pump properly.
1981	Richard L. Saxton	Received a patent for a tissue dispenser for telephone booths.
1986	Carter, Weiner, Youmans	Received a patent for a distributed pulse-forming network for magnetic modulators.
1987	Dixon, AuCoin, Malik	Received a patent for a monolithic planar doped barrier.
1988	Bertram O. Fraser-Reid	Biochemist at Duke University, develops and patents a method for linking simple sugars together to form oligasaccharides, compounds that are vitally important in regulating various biological activities.

ACKNOWLEDEMENTS:

First, and foremost I want to thank GOD.

For without his grace and mercy I wouldn't exist…

Then I want to thank my mother Gladys (ward) Stevenson

My immediate family Denise Brown, Deborah Igram, Asia, Ashley, Ernes, Crystal, Shakeyma, Shay Michael, Aaron, Anton, lil. Jesse Lee Baines, Courtney, Paige, and Devon… And Andrea

Desmona, Kurt, Keedo, Shirley, Tommy McFarland, junior, Sheila, Selina, Angelo,

Jessie Lyons, sistagail, Tony, Butch, junior, Brenda, Joe, North Carolina Family,

Mamie Ruth Ward my number 1 grandmother, All theWards, Fords, Williams', Pitts', Pittmans', Davis',

Rocky Mount, and Wilson(NC) I love Yall….

my Wyld Style Fam., R.I.P. DJ Lucky,

D-man fluid, Troof, Mjaye, H.B., Memphis Mike,Price, YT, Atl,

Venice Beach Crew

Najea, LifeDon, Hook, Shakell, Saltysalt, Sweet P,

Starbucks Chess Players,

Maniac, Gina Banic, and to Caroline Wolf who was of great importance in my book, and in my life